Friendship in an Age of Economics

Friendship in an Age of Economics

Resisting the Forces of Neoliberalism

Todd May

LEXINGTON BOOKS
Lanham • Boulder • New York • Toronto • Plymouth, UK

Published by Lexington Books
A wholly owned subsidiary of The Rowman & Littlefield Publishing Group, Inc.
4501 Forbes Boulevard, Suite 200, Lanham, Maryland 20706
www.rowman.com

10 Thornbury Road, Plymouth PL6 7PP, United Kingdom

British Library Cataloguing in Publication Information Available

Library of Congress Cataloging-in-Publication Data

The hardback edition of this book was previously cataloged by the Library of Congress as follows:

May, Todd, 1955–
Friendship in an age of economics : resisting the forces of neoliberalism / Todd May. p. cm.
p. cm.
Includes bibliographical references and index.
1. Interpersonal relations—Philosophy. 2. Friendship—Political aspects. 3. Friendship—Economic
aspects. 4. Neoliberalism. 5. Economics—Sociological aspects. I. Title.
HM1161.M39 2012
302—dc23
2012007554

ISBN: 978-0-7391-7581-1 (cloth : alk. paper)
ISBN: 978-0-7391-9284-9 (pbk.   )
ISBN: 978-0-7391-7582-8 (electronic)

Printed in the United States of America

Contents

Acknowledgments

This little book has its roots in an online reading and discussion group of two I have had the privilege to conduct with Ladelle McWhorter over the past several years. We have wrestled with the question of the character of neoliberalism: what it is, what it does, what it makes of us. Eventually I began to wonder how we might discover ways to live around or outside of neoliberalism aside from the traditional political categories of resistance. It is here that the idea of thinking about friendship arose: I believe, and I hope the manuscript presents a case for this, that neoliberalism is destructive of deep or close friendships. Alternatively, I think that such friendships challenge neoliberalism: Those are the stakes of this book.

I could not have come to even the limited understanding of neoliberalism that I possess without those bi-weekly sessions with Del. In addition, several other people read parts of the manuscript and offered immensely helpful suggestions: Dick Bernstein, Chris Grau, my wife Kathleen, and Stephanie Wakefield. I also had the opportunity to present a paper that is an early version of what appears here under the title "Friendship as Resistance" to audiences at the New School for Social Research, King's College at the University of Ontario, Manchester Metropolitan University, and at my home institution of Clemson University.

Finally, I was aided in this project by a sabbatical granted me by Clemson University. During that time, through the generosity of Simon Critchley and the faculty of the philosophy department of the New School, I was offered a course to teach and enough money to live for several months in New York while I finished the manuscript. During that time I was treated royally by many people at the New School, no one more so that Chiara Bottici, who, with her husband Benoit Challand, took me in as family.

This book is dedicated to my wife and (now grown) children: Kathleen, David, Rachel, and Joel. Daily they teach me the meaning of words like friendship and love.

ONE

Neoliberalism

These are difficult times. Some would say they are dark times. As I write these lines, in the fall of 2010, unemployment in the United States is just under 10 percent. Countless people have lost their homes in the wake of the bursting of the housing bubble. The environment, through global warming and depleted resources, is threatening to take revenge on us for nearly two centuries of exploitation. Anger toward immigrants and members of other religions are poisoning our social relations and increasing xenophobia. Political polarization is decreasing trust not only in politicians but in the very processes of governance, leading to parties of rage like the Tea Party. The news media, which was once seen as a check on public abuse and the informal conscience of the citizenry, is now viewed as little more than either a mouthpiece for the left or right or a form of sensationalized entertainment.

This book is not another record of these dark times. It does not offer an analysis of how we came to this pass. It does not add to the literature on how to bring us back into the light. Its aim is a little more intimate. The topic of this book is not something that appears in the news or in most of the popular books that are being written about what appears in the news. It is instead about who we are, with ourselves and one another.

Part of the goal of these pages is to show how who we are, with ourselves and one another, is a product of our times, these times. In this sense, what is under consideration is linked to the ills I recounted a moment ago. In another sense, however, the phenomena we encounter here are deeper and more insidious than some of these ills. They will not pass with the turning of the economic cycle, and will likely survive the current xenophobia and particular expressions of political polarization. (Unfortunately, they will not likely outlast the environmental crises.) It may seem, then, that my theme is yet another lament in the litany that

1

surrounds us. "Here is another problem you hadn't yet noticed, a blight upon our character and our relations."

This would be, given the structure of this book, roughly a third right. The first part of the book is an analysis of the deleterious character of who we have been encouraged to be, particularly over the past thirty or forty years. It discusses two types of people, two *figures* as I will call them (in an echo of the historian and philosopher Michel Foucault) that, to one extent or another, many of our dominant practices seek to make of us. These two figures, the consumer and the entrepreneur, both stem from and reinforce some of the root causes of our current ills. And they will likely persist beyond at least some of those ills, contaminating our relations with one another and buttressing the root cause of many of the practices and institutions that plague us. If our days have become difficult ones, there are reasons for this. And if we are to overcome our difficulties, we cannot escape looking at those reasons.

On the other hand, at the level at which I am looking at our times—that of our relations with one another—the news is not all bad. Not nearly so. Alongside whom we are often fabricated to be with ourselves and one another are ways of being that refuse that fabrication. These forms of refusal are as deeply woven into our character, and in many ways more deeply so, than the figures of the consumer and the entrepreneur. The focus here will be on one of those ways of being: friendship. We will see that certain kinds of friendship cut against consumerism and entrepreneurship, making us deeper and richer than these figures would have us be. Moreover, they also cut against the structure of practices that give rise to these figures, a structure that I will call, for lack of a better term, *neoliberalism*. I do not want to say that the forms of friendship I will describe here are the only ways in which our interpersonal relations resist neoliberalism and its figures. I will not, for instance, say much about love outside its place in friendship, as important as that is. However, I hope to offer some reflection on an arena of our lives that is central to who we are and to how we can begin to see beyond the difficulties into which we have been led.

Our relationships with one another, then, are a site of a struggle. The struggle is between who we are asked to be and who we might otherwise be—and often are. To understand this struggle requires two tasks. The first one consists in understanding the alternative to the figures of neoliberalism. We need a reflection on the nature of friendship. This is the topic of the second chapter of the book. Its task is philosophical: to ask what friendship is, to distinguish different types of friendship, and to locate the elements of friendship that might serve as alternatives to the figures of neoliberalism. When I say that the task is philosophical, however, I do not want to say that it is abstract, or, in particular, that it is abstracted from our lives. What I hope to describe is something that we will likely recognize. This is not to say that we have already thought about it all.

Before embarking on this book I certainly did not think about many of the themes that will arise in what follows. In fact, much of the philosophy that moves me does so by teaching me something that I recognize when it is said although I hadn't thought of it beforehand. It often appears to me as something I should have said, or wish I had said. In this case, of course, I would like to say it myself.

We might know what friendship is, however, and not know how it might confront the figures of neoliberalism. That is the theme of the third chapter. There are two forms that confrontation takes, although the first form is probably better described as a divergence rather than a confrontation. Certain types of friendship, because of their character, erect an alternative to the figures of neoliberalism. They resist those figures not through an active form of confrontation, but rather by being models of how one might live otherwise than how neoliberalism insists that we live. They are paths outside some of the practices that seek to dominate us. The other form is more overtly political. These types of friendship, or at least some among them, can form the basis for political solidarity. That solidarity in turn can be mobilized in resistance to or confrontation of the practices of neoliberalism itself. To be sure, many of the readers of this book will never be engaged in a movement of political solidarity. However, the friendships in which we are immersed often have elements that are continuous with healthy solidarity movements. The third chapter hopes to show the bond between how we resist the figures of neoliberalism in our certain of our friendships and how one can create political struggle against neoliberalism and its various products. Therefore, even if one does not consider herself to be political, it might be possible to recognize the affinity between one's life and those who struggle on certain stages in the political arena. Although friendships often aren't in themselves very political, they have themes that nourish some of the best political alliances.

If we are to understand how friendship may challenge the time we live in, however, we need to understand more about that time. I have used the term *neoliberalism* to describe our current period, or at least to give a label to one of its dominant motifs. It is a placeholder word, a word that makes it easy to refer to a group of related phenomena without having to list and repeat them every time I want to gesture at the set of themes against which friendship can press. I certainly do not want the term to be taken as a summation of *all* of the themes characteristic of our time. I don't believe that there is a single rubric, or even a group of related rubrics, that can do that. Michel Foucault, whom I mentioned above and whose writings and lectures will make periodic appearances in these pages, insists that there is no single theme or set of themes to which a historical period can be reduced. There is no Archimedean point that, if we can just take hold of it, will offer us leverage to a complete understanding of where we are now. This does not mean, however, that everything about us is equally important. What I am calling *neoliberalism* is an emerging and intersecting set of practices, embedded in a particular economic orientation, that has contributed much into making us who we are today. If we are to understand a central aspect of who we are, and of the difficulty and perhaps even the darkness of who we are asked to be, then we must come to grips with neoliberalism.

Neoliberalism can be a confusing term, not least because many people who are neoliberals are also neoconservatives. Moreover, as we unfold the themes and practices I want to isolate by invoking this term, I will refer to effects and aspects of neoliberalism that are often not directly associated with its use. However, at a first go, we might define neoliberalism as the view, dominant in many circles over the past thirty or forty years, that an unfettered (or largely unfettered) capitalist market is the best and most efficient way for an economy to be run. The degree to which an economy must be unfettered is a matter of debate, but at the very least neoliberalism rejects what might be called the welfare state capitalism of the post-World War II period up to roughly 1980. It holds that, rather than relying on the government to ensure the welfare of its citizens, a country must instead rely on the mechanisms of a capitalist market. If we were to invoke names here, we might say that neoliberalism represents the rejection of Keynesian economics in favor of something more akin to the views Milton Friedman and the Chicago School.

Here is a simple story one might tell about the rise of neoliberalism.

Keynesian economics emerged as itself a rejection of an earlier, liberal economics of the type broadly supported by today's neoliberals. John Maynard Keynes argued that governments periodically need to intervene in the market in order to stimulate demand. Specifically, during times in which people are either afraid to spend money or have no money to spend, the government needs to step in and fill the void by spending money itself.[1] This is because if nobody is spending, then jobs will be lost. And if jobs are lost, then there will be even less spending. All of this leads to a vicious cycle. To reverse the cycle, the government needs to spend money, even money it might not have at the moment, in order to create the jobs that will increase demand, which in turn will create more jobs. In this way, the government can bolster the economy, and will itself be able to make up its own spent money when the increase in jobs eventually increases a country's tax base.

This economic view was embraced during the Great Depression by the Roosevelt administration. It led to the various public works programs that came to be called the New Deal. Retrospectively, many economists credited the New Deal with helping the economy of the United States get back on its feet. This crediting was not universal. However, there was enough of a consensus on the effectiveness of Keynesian economics to make it the dominant economic approach for roughly forty years, until the early to middle 1970s. At that time, the US economy underwent a period of what came to be known as *stagflation*, which is a combination of a stagnant economy and inflation. Stagflation seemed to go against the predictions of Keynesian economics, which would argue that inflation would be associated with an expanding economy, not a stagnant one. The reason for this is that inflation occurs under conditions of increasing demand. But demand increases when people are spending money. And if people are spending money, then the economy can't be stagnant.

One explanation for the failure of the Keynesian prediction, although it is not the only one, refers to the effect of the Arab oil embargo of 1973. When the Arab oil-producing countries decided collectively to raise the price of crude oil, this caused significant inflation in oil-importing countries, like the US. However, the money spent on oil went out of the country. Rather than spurring economic development in the US, it was, from the perspective of the US economy, lost. So there was inflation and economic stagnation at the same time. From this perspective, the weakness of the Keynesian view lies in its assumption that national economies are closed loops, that is, that money spent in a particular national economy will stay in that national economy. When that is the case, inflation will be correlated with an expanding economy. But in a global economy, that assumption doesn't hold.

This alleged weakness in Keynesian economics allowed an opening for neoliberal theory, which could claim that it was better suited to a globalized marketplace. For neoliberals, governments are not efficient at intervening in the market. Instead, the role of governments should be to ensure that markets can operate so as to find their own equilibrium. Government intervention in the economy, especially by means of government spending, will only artificially alter, and therefore distort, the more efficient mechanisms of the capitalist market. This does not mean that government has no economic role to play. Rather, it must play the role of ensuring that markets can operate in an unfettered way, actively removing obstacles to their proper operation.

While classical liberal economic theory focused on the efficiencies of the market, current neoliberalism applies a similar argument regarding international trade. If a market, at least in theory, tends toward an equilibrium of supply and demand, so does international trade, and for the same reasons. Suppose, for instance, that the US has a certain technological know-how but another country has a pool of cheaper labor. That technological know-how will be invested in the country with the cheaper labor, resulting in jobs and therefore greater standard of living for the workers in the latter country, and cheaper prices for those purchasing the good that is produced. To be sure, this happens at the expense of what would have been better paid workers in the US. But those workers have options. Either they can choose to work for less money or they can re-tool themselves to fit in to the technologically more advanced society in which they live. In any case, the neoliberal argument is not that everyone is a winner all the time, but that resources are allocated in the most efficient manner not only in a national market but also in a globalized world. This point has been emphasized by Jagdish Bhagwati in his book *In Defense of Globalization*: "trade enhances growth, and. . . growth reduces poverty."[2]

All of what I have just said makes it sound as though neoliberalism makes its case solely as matter of economic efficiency. It does not. It is also, in its own view, a matter of freedom. In his classic defense of what he calls *liberalism* and what we have labeled *neoliberalism*, Milton Friedman writes, "Economic arrangements play a dual role in the promotion of a free society. On the one hand, freedom in economic arrangements is an end in itself. In the second place, economic freedom is also an indispensable means toward the achievement of political freedom."[3] If we hold freedom to be a value, then we have a reason to embrace neoliberalism. It allows people to act in accordance with their own desires rather than having their actions constrained or dictated by the government. This is not because the government does not act at all. Rather, it is because the government does not intervene in such a way as to make it easier or harder for people to choose one job or consumer good over another. For instance, if governmental action were to invest in propping up a failed corporation (a move that Friedman opposed with the bailout of Chrysler in 1979), it would be artificially competing with other corporations in that industry, and also inducing demand where it would not otherwise exist. All of this restrains the freedom of people to enter and exit the market on their own terms as well as creating inefficiencies in the market by preventing it from reaching its natural equilibrium.

The story I have just told here is one that would be embraced by many neoliberals. For some, it is not sympathetic enough to neoliberalism. For instance, Friedman would have argued that my discussion of Keynesian economics misdiagnosed the cause of the Great Depression, which was not a problem of demand but rather of the misapplication of monetary policy. "Had the money stock been kept from declining, as it clearly could and should have been," he writes of the period from 1929–1933, "the contraction would have been both shorter and far milder."[4] However, the two key elements justifying neoliberalism—economic efficiency and freedom—are mainstays of neoliberal thought. Moreover, that thought has gained traction as increased economic globalization has made it more difficult to apply economic policy within the closed borders of a polity.

That is one story that might be told about neoliberalism. There are other stories, however, that are less sympathetic.

One of these other stories comes from a trenchant Marxist critic of neoliberalism, David Harvey. Harvey argues that the rhetoric of freedom used to justify neoliberalism is actually a cover for a more insidious project, that of transferring wealth from the middle and lower classes back to the upper class. In *A Brief History of Neoliberalism*, he details the emergence of neoliberalism, tracing its roots not only in the classic cases of Chile, Great Britain, and the US, but also more locally in the response to New York's financial crisis in 1975. He shows how welfare capitalism, what he calls *embedded* capitalism, was able to spread a certain degree of general wealth at the expense of wresting profits from large corporations. However, over the course of the 1970s, welfare capitalism began to experience a series of difficulties, perhaps most seriously the Arab oil embargo of 1973. Alongside these difficulties, beginning with the imposition of neoliberal economics in Chile after the 1973 overthrow of Salvador Allende, a trend toward neoliberalism took place that returned the distribution of wealth to something more like a pre-welfarist pattern. Harvey writes, "We can, therefore, interpret neoliberalization as either a *utopian* project to realize a theoretical design for the reorganization of international capitalism or as a *political* project to re-establish the conditions for capital accumulation and to restore the power of economic elites. In what follows I shall argue that the second of these objectives has in practice dominated."[5]

We should be clear about the alternatives Harvey has placed before us. The first alternative concerns neoliberal theory. It is roughly the idea that if we allow free markets to operate in a relatively unimpeded way, we will generate the most wealth and distribute it in the most efficient way. Although, as Harvey points out, there are theoretical tensions within this utopian alternative (for example a critique of state power alongside a demand that the state be powerful enough to protect property rights), it has been presented as an attractive alternative to what appeared to be the failing underpinnings of Keynesian economics. The alternative explanation, the one Harvey favors, is that of a restoration of class power. In this explanation, neoliberal theory is presented as a justification for the return of capital accumulation; however, its function is solely ideological. The reality lies with the restoration of capital, not with the generation of wealth or the efficiency of distributions.

Naomi Klein's *The Shock Doctrine*, like Harvey's *Brief History*, offers an account of the emergence of neoliberalism over the past several decades.[6] Her framework differs from Harvey's in relying more on the imposition of theory than on the action of classes. It is not that she thinks the economic elites have had nothing to do with neoliberalism's rise. Far from it. However, she places more importance on theory, and particularly on the theory and uses of Milton Friedman's market libertarianism.

In a nutshell, Klein argues that the spread of Friedman's theory, particularly through his acolytes in and around the University of Chicago, occurred through various type of shock therapy. Just as electroshock therapy renders a patient disoriented and therefore unable to resist outside intervention, economic shock therapy renders populations disoriented and unable to resist the imposition of neoliberal market reforms. Thus,

in the first experiment in neoliberal economics, Pinochet's Chile was par-
alyzed when the government of Salvador Allende was overthrown and
martial law declared. This allowed Friedman's students not only to over-
turn Allende's mild socialist reforms, but to turn Chile into a laboratory
for Friedman's theory. The Chilean experiment has since been repeated
in Argentina, Poland, Russia, South Africa, and, to a lesser extent, in the
US and UK. There has been a collusion of right wing think tanks and
economic elites that have imposed Friedman's theory and in turn benefitted from it, even though, as Klein shows, many of the policies stemming
from this theory have been so disastrous that they have had to be either
eliminated or at least softened in their effects.

One might read Klein, like Harvey, as arguing that the use of Friedman's utopian views is simply a cover for what Harvey calls a political
class project. However, we need not do so. We can read Klein as intro-
ducing the idea that the imposition of neoliberal reforms was not entirely
a cynical project, but instead the enterprise of people who really believed
in the virtues of what later came to be called neoliberalism. Granted, their
methods were harsh and even cruel, but that does not diminish the idea
that they believed in what they were doing. Taken this way, we can begin
to explain the rise of neoliberalism without having to resort to anything
like a class strategy to explain it. Her explanation does not exclude the
presence of class interests, and she certainly details the deleterious effects
of neoliberalism on the majority of those upon whom it was imposed.
However, her emphasis on the imposition of theory leans less heavily on
the idea, embraced by Harvey, that theory is merely a cover for a project
that had no belief in what it preached.

Harvey's and Klein's assessment of neoliberalism is in stark contrast
to that of its promoters such as Friedman and Jagdish Baghwati.[7] Ultimately, our interest is less in the fortunes of neoliberalism than in the
kinds of figures it creates, the types of lives it encourages us to lead.
However, the question of how we are encouraged to live is not separate
from the question of who benefits from our being encouraged to live in
that way. This is not to say that the beneficiaries of the figures of neoliberalism—the consumer and the entrepreneur—are created by those who
might benefit, that is, consciously and for the sake of their benefitting.
There is no conspiracy at work in the creation of the figures of neoliberalism.

Rather, the idea is something like this. If one benefits from the way the
world is arranged, one will have no motivation to change it. In fact, one
will hardly have reason to take a deep notice of the arrangement itself.
Everything will be going along swimmingly, and there will be no cause
for reflection. It is similar to when one gets in one's car, turns on the
ignition, and the car starts. One doesn't notice the car, and feels no need
to tamper with it. One doesn't even think about the car, until it stops
working for some reason or another. The car is just there at the edges of

one's consciousness. For those who benefit from neoliberalism, the situation is much the same. They don't notice neoliberalism as such. They just go to work each day without a sense that there's anything in the current social, political, or especially economic situation that needs to be fixed. The difference is that if those who benefit from neoliberalism are those with great power to begin with, this will serve to keep the current arrangements in place. It is not that there is a conspiracy to benefit those with power; rather, it's that, from the perspective of those with power, those in the best position to affect economic and political arrangements, there just isn't anything wrong.

If those in power benefit from a world in which we are encouraged to be consumers and entrepreneurs, we can expect that these figures would likely be more entrenched and less likely to be uprooted. And so it would be worth pausing over the current legacy of neoliberalism, to ask whom it benefits and at whose expense. Is it the case, as neoliberals are wont to argue, that unrestrained markets create a rising tide that lifts all boats, or at least most of them? Or are some boats lifted higher than others? Or, instead, are some boats well aloft while others are left to sink?

The record does not speak well for the proponents or neoliberalism, either with respect to the relation of freedom to neoliberalism or to the ability of neoliberalism to spread wealth in a globalized world. Regarding freedom, the obvious current counterexample we could raise is that of China, where a broadly capitalist market is combined with a repressive state apparatus. One might object to the example of China, since it does not embrace neoliberalism uncritically. For instance, as Joseph Stiglitz points out, China rejected the IMF prescriptions for loans during the 1980s.[8] In addition, as I write these lines, there is a debate raging about China's policy of keeping its exports up by artificially lowering its currency through the purchase of foreign currency. These are reasonable objections, and it would be going too far to say that China embraces neoliberalism unambiguously.[9] However, the example of China shows that a country can move from a state-owned economy to a capitalist one without increasing the level of political freedom its people might enjoy.

The more damning example is that of Pinochet's Chile. The reason it is more damning is that when Augusto Pinochet, with the assistance of the CIA,[10] overthrew the partially socialist government of Salvador Allende, he imported economists from the Chicago School (about whom we will have more to say later in this chapter) in order to turn Chile into a laboratory for neoliberal economics. The Pinochet regime was notorious for its repressive policies, crushing any dissent ruthlessly. Thousands of people were tortured and disappeared. Any discontent with government policies was crushed. And yet, at least in the initial years of the Pinochet regime, economic policy was not only in line with that advocated by Friedman and the Chicago School; it was being run by Chicago School economists themselves.

Who benefits from the dominance of neoliberal economic policy? David Harvey provides some illuminating statistics in this regard. "After the implementation of neoliberal policies in the late 1970s, the share of national income of the top 1 per cent of income earners in the US soared, to reach 15 percent (very close to its pre–Second World War share) by the end of the century. The top 0.1 per cent of income earners in the US increased their share of the national income from 2 per cent in 1978 to over 6 per cent by 1999, while the ratio of the median compensation of workers to the salaries of CEOs increased from just over 30 to 1 in 1970 to nearly 500 to 1 by 2000."[11] This shifting of income did not only occur in the US. Britain, under the guidance of Prime Minister Margaret Thatcher, was another major bastion of early neoliberalism. There, "the top 1 per cent of income earners in Britain have doubled their share of the national income from 6.5 per cent to 13 per cent since 1982."[12] As Harvey points out, similar shifts occurred in other countries that adopted neoliberal policies of deregulation, privatization, and decreased government involvement in the social sector.

The fact that the upper classes benefit from neoliberal policies does not, by itself, show that everyone else loses. Economics does not have to be a zero-sum game. Perhaps the benefits accrued by the upper classes were in their turn invested in the economy, bringing wealth to everyone. Or perhaps there was a general rise in wealth, so that even if the upper classes got a greater share of the national income, the absolute level for everyone else also rose. This, however, turns out not to be the case. In 2006, the *New York Times* reported:

> Over all, average incomes rose 27 percent in real terms over the quarter-century from 1979 through 2004. But the gains were narrowly concentrated at the top and offset by losses for the bottom 60 percent of Americans, those making less than $38,761 in 2004. The bottom 60 percent of Americans, on average, made less than 95 cents in 2004 for each dollar they reported in 1979, analysis of the I.R.S. data shows. The next best-off group, the fifth of Americans on the 60th to 80th rungs of the income ladder, averaged 2 cents more income in 2004 for each dollar they earned in 1979. Only those in the top 5 percent had significant gains. The average income of those on the 95th to 99th rungs of the income ladder rose by 53 percent, almost twice the average rate.[13]

If we turn from the US to Third World countries, the situation is even more bleak. The economist Ha-Joon Chang notes the following:

> Since the 1980s, however, when the continent embraced neo-liberalism, Latin America has been growing less than one-third of the rate of the "bad old days" [the preceding period focused on internal economic development]. Even if we discount the 1980s as a decade of adjustment and take it out of the equation, *per capita* income in the region during the 1990s grew at basically half the rate of the "bad old days" (3.1% vs. 1.7%). Between 2000 and 2005, the region has done even worse; it virtu-

ally stood still, with *per capita* income growing at only 0.6% per year. As for Africa, its *per capita* income grew relatively slowly even in the 1960s and the 1970s (1–2% a year). But since the 1980s, the region has seen a *fall* in living standards.[14]

Chang is not an economist who comes from the left. Instead, he favors capitalist development with an emphasis on internal growth, as happened in his native South Korea. Neither is the International Monetary Fund itself. In 2003, in an occasional paper published on its website entitled "Effects of Financial Globalization on Developing Countries," its authors note that "From the perspective of macroeconomic stability, consumption is regarded as a better measure of well-being than output; fluctuations in consumption are therefore regarded as having negative impacts on economic welfare. There is little evidence that financial integration has helped developing countries to better stabilize fluctuations in consumption growth. . . In fact, new evidence presented in this paper suggests that low to moderate levels of financial integration may have made some countries subject to greater volatility of consumption relative to that of output."[15]

Assessments from the left are, unsurprising, just as grim. Mike Davis, author of *Planet of Slums*, notes that,

> Urban Africa and Latin America were the hardest hit by the artificial depression engineered by the IMF and the White House—indeed in many countries the economic impact of the SAPs [the structural adjustment programs insisted upon by the IMF that required the implementation of neoliberal programs in return for IMF loans and World Bank economic support] during the 1980s, in tandem with protracted drought, rising oil prices, soaring interest rates, and falling commodity prices, was more severe and long-lasting than the Great Depression. Third World cities, especially, were trapped in a vicious cycle of increasing immigration, decreasing formal employment, falling wages, and collapsing revenues. The IMF and World Bank, as we have seen, promoted regressive taxation through public-service user fees for the poor, but made no counterpart effort to reduce military expenditure or to tax the incomes of the rich.[16]

I could go on.[17] The dominance of neoliberal policies over the course of the past thirty years has left the rich in a far better situation than the middle classes or the poor, and has rendered the poor far more vulnerable than they had been under earlier economic policies. Moreover, this shift has not been accompanied by economic growth. If anything, the situation has been the opposite.

One might wonder why, given this legacy of neoliberalism, there has not been a resistance to its continued imposition. There has been. In Latin America particularly, the elections over the past decade of progressive, anti-neoliberal governments in Ecuador, Brazil, Venezuela, Argentina, and Bolivia have demonstrated that many countries have had enough of neoliberalism, and would prefer governmental interventions that favor the majority of their citizens. There have been strikes in France and elsewhere against the imposition of particular neoliberal policies. (However, as I write this, the current President of France, Nicolas Sarkozy, is an unabashed supporter of neoliberalism.) In most industrial countries, however, and particularly in the United States, there has not been a concerted effort to resist neoliberal policy. There have certainly been criticisms of greed on Wall Street, particularly in the wake of the recession that has been with us since 2008. And there have been occasional critiques, from both left and right, of governmental support for elites at the expense of the rest of the citizenry. But these critiques have not been directed against the policies of neoliberalism itself, except perhaps from the left margins of mainstream discourse. In fact, on the right there has been a call for less governmental intervention, a policy that would seem to support rather than challenge neoliberal policy.

This muted, or at times even supportive, reaction to neoliberalism would seem to be a puzzle. Why support something whose effects are deleterious to most of us? Why allow a free reign to economic elites whose activities seem to be directed toward, or at the very least have resulted in, their enrichment at the expense of everyone else? This would seem to call for an explanation. There are, in all likelihood, several factors that would help explain this puzzle. One might suggest that particularly in a globalized world, people feel more hopeless about the prospects for change. This is something I see among my students at Clemson University. Granted, since I teach in a philosophy program and also have a reputation for being well left of center politically, I tend to draw students that one would not tend to characterize as representative of the mainstream of college students. However, I do draw students who think there is something wrong with the world and would like to change it. Many of these students express a desire for a different world, and are particularly concerned about the focus on material gain that they see going on around them. But they do not know what to do about it. They feel small and ineffective in the face of the problems confronting them. They are idealistic, but they lack hope.

Neoliberalism contributes to this through its intersection with globalization. Recall that for Bahgwati, one of the great virtues of globalization is international trade and economic interaction. A central characteristic of neoliberalism is the emergence of corporations that are not merely multinational, but transnational. They have no particular home, but instead exist everywhere. The critic Masao Miyoshi insists that we must distinguish the older multinational corporation from the emerging transnational corporation, pointing out that "a multinational corporation (MNC) is one that is headquartered in a nation, operating in a number of countries. . . [and is] finally tied to the home nation. A truly transnational corporation, on the other hand, might no longer be tied to its nation of origin but is adrift and mobile, ready to settle anywhere and exploit any state including its own, as long as the affiliation serves its own interest."[18] Transnational corporations answer to no national entity. If a national (or local) political entity makes things inconvenient for them, they simply relocate. This makes it more difficult to confront economically based exploitation and oppression. In fact, neoliberalism undercuts solidarity and promotes discord. If workers threaten to organize for better conditions, companies simply have to threaten to move somewhere else, somewhere that has a more compliant workforce. (Among the places we see the effects of this aspect of neoliberalism is in the rising xenophobia of many Western countries, whose workers are afraid that "they are taking our jobs.") Because of the difficulties of confronting transnational corporations and other entities, hopelessness can take hold among those who dissent from the current order of things.

The failure of hope is one reason for the lack of resistance to neoliberalism. But there is more than just hopelessness. Hopelessness alone does not explain the fact that there is often an active embrace of many neoliberal doctrines. Take, for instance, the current popularity in the US of the Tea Party. It may be a passing phenomenon (time will tell), but its rejection of what it sees as the domination by the elites of the economic order is not a call for any kind of social control. It is, instead, a demand for more individualism, for less government intervention into the economic lives of people. According to Tea Party supporters, the proper role of government is to refrain from intervening into the economy. It should allow the economy, in the form of individual initiative and choice, to operate on its own principles. The Tea Party rejects Keynesian measures such as deficit spending and job creation programs.

Although much of the Tea Party's core consists of those who are economically well off and stand to benefit from neoliberal doctrine,[19] there is currently much more widespread support for its positions, especially its economic ones. Distrust and fear of government is rampant. What is remarkable, however, about this distrust and fear is not that it exists—times are difficult, after all—but that the proposed solution for the problems associated with government is to endorse the very economic policies that have brought us to this pass. As we have seen, neoliberalism has not benefitted many of those who demand its continuance, if not in name then certainly in content. It has harmed them. Why do so many people want more of it?

Part of the answer—only part, but, I believe, a significant part—lies in what neoliberalism has made of us.

People are, no doubt, partly products of their time. Not just now, but always. This is not to say that we are wholly in thrall to the conditions that surround us, or that we are utterly determined by the context in which we live. If that were the case, there would never be social change or advance; or at least, if there were, it would come about independent of human reflection and intervention. Rather, the idea is that who we are is not *independent* of the time in which we live. We are not simply the children of our age, but neither are we simply its parents. Who we are and who we become cannot be divorced from the context in which we become who we are. We must address, in one way or another, the challenges it confronts us with and, more deeply, the terms in which it issues those challenges. We are not immune to the ways problems are posed or lives are sought to be molded at a given moment. We may challenge those ways and those moldings, but even then, it is *those* ways and moldings—and the current thinking about them—that are challenged, and not others.

This is not difficult to see. In a famous story, the Catholic inquisitors of Galileo refused to look through his telescope to determine whether the earth revolved around the sun, instead putting him on trial and requiring that he recant his heliocentrism. It is a story not lost upon the philosopher Descartes, who wrote in a letter in the wake of the trial, "the desire that I have to live in peace and continue the life I have embarked on, taking as my device the motto: *he lives well who hides well*, means that I am happy to be freed from the fear I had of acquiring, by means of my writing, more knowledge than I desire. . ."[20] More recently, at least in much of the world, controversial scientific claims would not be subject to trial and potential imprisonment. The reception of Darwin's theory of natural selection displays this change. It is not that his theory goes unchallenged in certain theological quarters. Rather, that challenge is—and was—to the theory itself. Darwin was not put on trial for it.[21] Darwin, and more recent scientists, live in a context in which scientific challenge costs much less than it once did. Further, that context is not one in which geocentrism, with all its cosmic and theological implications, is the order of the day. We are no longer circumscribed by the particular doctrines with their particular sanctions that defined an earlier era.

Moreover, not all of us do seek to challenge our contexts. Most of the time we seek to be able to live, to get by, and to make something significant of ourselves and our relationships with others within the terms our times offer to us. Just as it is true that most of us do not exist solely as products of our time, it is also true that most of us do not raise a banner against it. We live within its parameters, and make of ourselves what we can.

Our time, this time, a time often dominated by what I have termed neoliberalism, has its own terms and conditions, and we are influenced and often molded by them. We are made to be who we are, and asked to live as we live, in a context largely provided by neoliberal thought and practice. Because of this, we must not see neoliberalism solely as an economic doctrine or even as a set of economic practices. When David Harvey calls neoliberalism "a *political* project to re-establish the conditions for capital accumulation and to restore the power of economic elites," he captures an important aspect of neoliberalism, but by no means all of it. To live within neoliberalism, a neoliberalism that has conditioned us for at least thirty to forty years, is to be immersed in a set of conditions that cannot help influencing how we think, feel, and act. There are different ways of conceiving this influence. The path we will follow here has been traced by Michel Foucault, who has discussed the influence of one's time on who one is in terms of the concept of *figures*.

NOTES

1. The central elements of Keynes' economic theory are to be found in Keynes, John Maynard, *The General Theory of Employment, Money, and Interest*(London: Macmillan, 2007 [1936]). For a good general summary of his views from a progressive perspective, see Hahnel, Robin, *The ABC's of Political Economy*. London: Pluto Press, 2003, chapter 6.

2. Bhagwati, Jagdish, *In Defense of Globalization* (Oxford: Oxford University Press, 2004), p. 53. This book is often anecdotal in its defense of a broadly neoliberal globalization in its ability to reduce poverty, enhance gender equality, and promote democracy. In what follows, we raise questions as to both the general efficiency and justice of neoliberal globalization.

3. Friedman, Milton, *Capitalism and Freedom* (Chicago: University of Chicago Press, 1962), p. 8.

4. *Capitalism and Freedom*, p. 50.

5. Harvey, David, *A Brief History of Neoliberalism* (Oxford: Oxford University Press, 2005), p. 19.

6. Klein, Naomi, *The Shock Doctrine: The Rise of Disaster Capitalism* (New York: Metropolitan Books, 2007).

7. See note 2, above.

8. Stiglitz, Joseph. *Globalization and its Discontents*. New York: W.W. Norton, 2002, pp. 181–87.

9. David Harvey offers a discussion of China's relation to neoliberalism in Chapter 5 of *A Brief History of Neoliberalism*.

10. The history of the CIA's involvement in the overthrow of the Allende government has been documented in many places. One helpful source is Part IV of Robert Johansen's *The National Interest and the Human Interest: An Analysis of U.S. Foreign Policy* (Princeton: Princeton University Press, 1980).

11. *A Brief History of Neoliberalism*, p. 16.

12. *A Brief History of Neoliberalism*, p. 17.

13. Johnston, David Cay, "'04 Income in U.S. Was Below 2000 Level," *New York Times*, November 28, 2006, www.nytimes.com/2006/11/28/business/28tax.html?_r=1 (accessed December 14, 2010)

14. Chang, Ha-Joon, *Bad Samaritans: The Myth of Free Trade and the Secret History of Capitalism* (London: Bloomsbury Press, 2008), p. 28.

15. Prasad, Eswar, Rogoff, Kenneth, Wei, Shang-Jin, and Kose, M. Ayan, "Effects of Financial Globalization on Developing Countries: Some Empirical Evidence," www.imf.org/external/np/res/docs/2003/031703.pdf (accessed October 12, 2010).

16. Davis, Mike, *Planet of Slums* (London: Verso Press, 2006), p. 155.

17. For instance, Naomi Klein details the deleterious effects of neoliberalism in Chile, Bolivia, Poland, and South Africa, among other places, in *The Shock Doctrine*. One could also consult Freeman, Alan, "Globalisation: Economic stagnation and divergence," in Pettifor, *A Real World Economic Outlook ₂* (Basingstoke: Palgrave MacMillan, 2003), pp. 152–59; Keating, M. F., "Globalisation and the Dynamics of Impoverishment," www.richmond.ac.uk/cms/pdfs/Keating%202001%20DSA%20Paper%20PDF.

pdf (accessed October 12, 2010), and Marfleet, Phil, "Globalisation and the Third World," http://pubs.socialistreviewindex.org.uk/isj81/marfleet.htm (accessed October 12, 2010).

18. Miyoshi, Masao, "A Borderless World? From Colonialism to Transnationalism and the Decline of the Nation-State," *Critical Inquiry*, Vol. 19, Summer 1993, p. 736.

19. For a profile of those who affiliate themselves with the Tea Party, see Montopoli, Brian, "Tea Party Supporters: Who They Are and What They Believe," *CBS News*, www.cbsnews.com/8301-503544_162-20002529-503544.html (accessed December 14, 2010)

20. Descartes, René, *Philosophical Essays and Correspondence.* ed. Roger Ariew (Indianapolis: Hackett, 2000), p. 44.

21. This does not mean that theological practice has entirely refrained from personal threats, as the fatwa against Salman Rushdie for his publication of *The Satanic Verses* attests.

TWO
Figures

What is a figure? Foucault utilizes the term in the first volume of *The History of Sexuality*, but he does not define it. He says that, "Four figures emerged from this preoccupation with sex, which mounted throughout the nineteenth century—four privileged objects of knowledge, which were also targets and anchorage points for the ventures of knowledge: the hysterical woman, the masturbating child, the Malthusian couple, and the perverse adult."[1] We will return to these four figures below. What we want now, though, is a working definition of the term *figure*.

We should note that figures are real, but they have single characteristics. They are, we might say, portraits of people painted in a single hue. But to say they are portraits is not to say that they simply represent people, or represent what they are like. They also *are* people. They are produced by their time, and, at least in the case of the four figures of sexuality, they become objects of a knowledge that at once creates and seeks to understand them. We might say of these figures that they are people inasmuch as those people embody certain characteristics produced by the time in which they live.

At first blush, this definition does not seem far from Max Weber's definition of what he calls an ideal type. "An idea type is formed by the one-sided *accentuation* of one or more points of view and by the synthesis of a great many diffuse, discrete, more or less present and occasionally absent *concrete individual* phenomena, which are arranged according to those one-sidedly emphasized viewpoints into an *analytical* construct."[2] However, there may be, depending on one's interpretation, an important distinction between them, one that would tilt us closer to the figure than to the ideal type.

Ideal types are not met within reality. "In its conceptual purity, this mental construct cannot be found empirically anywhere in reality."[3] In-

17

stead, the ideal type is a theme that is more or less instantiated or expressed in particular individuals. "It has the significance of a purely ideal
limiting concept with which the real situation or action is *compared* and
surveyed for the explication of certain of its significant components."[4]
Capitalism, for instance, is an ideal type. There is no purely capitalist
economy, so the historian or social scientist analyzing a particular situation introduces the concept as an analytical tool, recognizing that every
concrete situation is only more or less capitalist.

By contrast to ideal types, figures are real, at least to an extent. They
are created and defined by the environment in which they arise. Often,
figures are given a label within that environment, as with the four figures
of sexuality. They are constructed, in Foucault's eyes, through a series of
practices that give rise to them by impinging upon individuals in particular ways. This distinguishes figures from ideal types in two ways, the
latter of which points to the deeper significance played by figures. The
first distinction is that figures are created within a situation, not by someone analyzing the situation from the outside. The hysterical woman, for
instance, is labeled as such by a practitioner, while capitalism, at least as
an analytic construct, an ideal type, is labeled by the historian or social
scientist who is attempting to understand that situation.

Second, and of more moment, ideal types are not normative. They are
not meant to judge or evaluate something as better or worse. Weber
insists that,"[W]e should emphasize that the idea of an ethical *imperative,*
of a "model" of what "ought" to exist is to be carefully distinguished
from the analytical construct, which is "ideal" in the strictly logical sense
of the term."[5] By contrast, figures are essentially normative. They do not
merely categorize; they also judge empirically. These judgments are not
always ideal in the sense of being positive. In fact, most figures are objects of a negative ethical judgment. But judged they are, and that is
essential to their operation. By being judged, a figure becomes subject to
certain practices of intervention, treatment, or recognition that reinforce
or attempt to eliminate (and often both at the same time) the characteristics associated with that figure. Because of this, a figure is labeled, created, molded, discussed, and impinged upon by those in the situation in
which she finds herself.

We should not take this to mean that a figure is nothing other than the
characteristics of that figure. A perverse adult is not only perverse. She is,
perhaps, also a laborer or a pool player or a church deacon or a baseball
fan. However, as a perverse adult, she is often thought of, above all these
other aspects of her life, as perverse.

To grasp the concept of the figure, we might first turn to an example
that Foucault provides in *Discipline and Punish,* that of the delinquent.
Although Foucault does not use the term *figure* in describing the delinquent, his treatment of it is the same as that of the four figures of sexual-

ity: as a person at once produced and known by the milieu in which she arises.

One might, of course, think that the concept of the delinquent exists independently of particular historical circumstances. Periodically, we refer to kids that always seem to be in trouble as "delinquents" (or, the same thing, as "juveniles"). These are people we think are likely to spend a good part of their future in jail. The term *delinquent*, however, has a stricter reference, one that arises in the course of the emergence of the modern prison and its associated social and political milieu. "[P]rison has succeeded extremely well in producing delinquency, a specific type, a politically or economically less dangerous—and, on occasion, usable—form of illegality; in producing delinquents, in an apparently marginal, but in fact centrally supervised milieu; in producing the delinquent as a pathologized subject."[6]

Who is the delinquent, this pathologized but periodically useful subject produced by the prison? Ostensibly the delinquent is the person who represents the failure of the prison. If the prison's goal is to reform someone and then return them to society as a normal individual, the delinquent—who keeps returning to prison after committing more crimes—indicates that the prison isn't working. However, that superficial impression is deceiving. The delinquent travels through spaces of illegality, offering opportunities for penal and social service authorities to monitor his or her activities, and through this monitoring to oversee to some extent the character of the criminal underworld. This oversight helps keep the lid on activities that resist the disciplinary goal of normalizing a population. (We will speak more of normalization in a moment.) On occasion, the delinquent can even be in overt cooperation with these authorities, acting as an informant or denouncing a rival to them.

The delinquent is an ironic character in the milieu of the prison. It might seem as though the delinquent, in refusing to be normalized, is a character of resistance to the prison. However, this resistance is itself, we might say, choreographed by the prison and its operation. Rather than resisting the prison and its disciplinary apparatus, the delinquent represents one of the ways in which resistance can become, if not co-opted, then at least channeled into acceptable forms. "[T]he existence of a legal prohibition creates around it a field of illegal practices, which one manages to supervise, while extracting from it an illicit profit through elements, themselves illegal, but rendered manipulable by their organization in delinquency. This organization is an instrument for administering and exploiting illegalities."[7] This is why Foucault says that the delinquent is produced by the prison system rather than created in opposition to it.

The delinquent, then, is, in a way, a real person. But why only *in a way*? There are two reasons, both of which will prove important for us in understanding the role friendship can and does play in our lives. First, except perhaps in very extreme cases (and even these are hard to conceive), delinquency, as we noted a moment ago regarding all figures, does not exhaust the description of any particular individual. A person may be a delinquent, but he or she is not just that and nothing more. That individual may also be a son, one who feels a deep affinity for a mother who suffered a broken life with an alcoholic husband. It may be someone who has an ambivalent but vital relationship with a friend or a lover. It could be someone who is also a good car mechanic or carpenter or brick layer. One may be a delinquent in a way in which one is not a Weberian particular ideal type, but one is (almost) never that alone.

The importance of this lies in the fact that however much we instantiate the figures of our time, there are always other aspects of us that are not reducible to those figures. There is always more to us, or at least potentially more, than any given set of forces impinging upon us might make of us. This is not to say that there is some reservoir of individuality that each of us possesses that remains untouched by our social surroundings. It is not to claim that our context can reach only so far and no further into our selves. It is not to say that there is something left over behind the ways in which we are molded, a something that some philosophers would want to call *free will*. The idea here is more modest than that. It is that any particular set of social forces that mold us into any particular figures does not exhaust who we are. What lies outside a particular molding may be another molding; the delinquent who is a brick layer or a carpenter has been subject to a different set of social forces in becoming those things. It may be that an individual is more than one figure at a given time, say a delinquent and (in another figure we will meet in a moment) a perverse adult. What needs to be emphasized is that people who are molded into particular figures are not flat or one-sided, not simply the figure they are molded to be. This is not because they exist outside all of the influence of their surroundings; it is because they are exposed to and must navigate through more than one set of those influences. This idea becomes crucial in the last part of this book when we discuss friendship as an alternative to the figures of neoliberalism.

The second reason a delinquent (or any other figure) is only *in a way* a real person is that the social forces that have made him a delinquent are themselves subject to critique and resistance. We might be tempted to think of the practices Foucault recounts in which delinquents are inscribed as irresistible forces, monolithic and invincible. This would be a mistake. Foucault, who was often characterized as a pessimist, once commented that, "My optimism would consist in saying, 'So many things can be changed, being as fragile as they are, tied more to contingencies than to necessities, more to what is arbitrary than to what is rationally established, more to complex but transitory historical contigencies than to inevitable anthropological constants. . .'"[8] If we are always in part a product of our times, we must recognize that are times are no more than that—historically situated times. They do not consist of cosmic forces that ineluctably make us what we are. The practices that mold us consist, as Foucault tells us, of contingencies. They can be recognized, confronted, and, perhaps with a little luck, changed. In many ways, many more than we are often aware, we do not have to be who we are. This is especially true of the figures generated during particular historical periods. This idea will also become crucial in the last part of the book when we discuss friendship as offering resources for resisting the figures of neoliberalism.

One might want to object to this last reason for claiming that, for instance, a delinquent is only so *in a way*. One might say instead that the delinquent really is a delinquent (or at least, respecting the first caveat, a delinquent to a certain extent), but only contingently so. One is a delinquent, but one might resist what has made her so. Fair enough. In saying that the practices that mold a society's particular figures are mutable, I am not saying that, for instance, the delinquent is not really one. Rather, my suggestion is that the delinquency into which she has been molded is not carved in stone. Although a delinquent, she might become something else: not by overcoming her delinquency, but by challenging the very conception of delinquency and its allied practices. By insisting that a delinquent is only *in a way* a delinquent, I want to insist that delinquency, or any other figure, is both *non-exhaustive* and *revisable*. There is always more to a delinquent than her delinquency, and the fact that one is a delinquent can itself be challenged by resisting the terms in which one has been cast. To anticipate, friendship can and often does occur outside the figures of the consumer and the entrepreneur, and it can challenge those figures in their influence on who we are and how we relate to one another.

The figures with which we are primarily concerned here are not the delinquent, but the consumer and the entrepreneur. It is they whom we have become and they who can be resisted through certain forms of friendship. But before we investigate these figures in depth, it would be worth pausing briefly over a previous set of figures: the four figures of sexuality that Foucault describes in the first volume of his history of sexuality. Not only do these figures themselves contrast with our more contemporary figures. Collectively, they revolve around a project—the project of normalization—that has receded in the face of the rise of neoliberalism. We will be able to understand the figures of neoliberalism in greater depth if we can see their distance from the project of normalization.

Foucault's discussion of the four figures of sexuality is brief, only a couple of pages. The figures themselves arise from what he calls *strategies* of sexualization that have their origin over a hundred years before the emergence of these figures, as early as the Counter-Reformation. However, it is in the nineteenth century that these strategies take on their full force. The first figure, the hysterical woman arises from "a threefold process whereby the feminine body was analyzed—qualified and disqualified—as being thoroughly saturated with sexuality; whereby it was integrated into the sphere of medical practices, by reason of a pathology intrinsic to it; whereby, finally, it was placed in organic communication with the social body. . . the family space. . . and the life of children."[9] The hysterical woman is the woman who, as mother, cannot entirely control her emotions; and this lack of control is related to her sexual instincts.

One might ask the question here of how the purported lack of control relates to sexual instincts. It is a question that goes to nineteenth- and early twentieth-century attitudes toward women as well as toward specific biological claims of the relation of sexuality to particular symptoms. For our purposes, that question is a bit wide of the point. What isn't wide of the point, though, is the general idea that sexuality has a deep tie to hysteria. In the first volume of *The History of Sexuality*, Foucault argues that over the course of the past several hundred years, our identity has become deeply tied to our sexuality. Who we are has come to be inseparable from the kinds of ways we embody and express our sexuality. In fact, the issue is even deeper than that. *Sex*, as a set of activities between bodies, has become *sexuality*, which is not simply corporeal or genital interaction but also and more important a psychological key to who we are. "So we must not refer a history of sexuality to the agency of sex; but rather show how 'sex' is historically subordinate to sexuality."[10] The modern touchstone for this view is, of course, Freud. However, Foucault claims that we can trace this view back to the revision of the confessional during the Counter-Reformation. That revision changed confessional practice from a confession of acts to one of desires, and, among those desires, made desires around sex central ones. "An imperative was established: Not only will you confess to acts contravening the law, but you will seek to transform your desire, your every desire, into discourse."[11] (An ironic element of this history is that it places Freud, the great antireligionist, in a historical line that renders his practice continuous with the Catholic confessional.)

The sexuality that is the hidden secret of hysteria is also the key to understand the masturbating child, the perverse adult, and the Malthusian couple. The masturbating child is "at the same time 'natural' and 'contrary to nature.'"[12] He or she is natural because the urge to masturbate, or more generally to respond to sexual urges, is innate. But at the same time these urges, if succumbed to, will warp the child's development. There must be a constant monitoring of children in order to prevent any indulgence in sexuality in order to assure the normal development of children. In his lecture series *Abnormal*, Foucault depicts some of the practices arising from this concern with childhood sexuality. For instance, in the nineteenth century a crusade against masturbation arose that required constant vigilance by parents. "Actually, the family must be a space of continual surveillance. Children must be watched over when they are washing, going to bed, getting up, and while they sleep. Parents must keep a lookout all around their children, over their clothes and bodies. . . If the child has a pale complexion, if his face is wan, if his eyelids are bluish or purple, if he has a certain languid look and has a tired or listless air about him when he leaves his bed, the reason is clear: masturbation."[13]

The perverse adult, unfortunately, remains among us: it is the figure of the person whose sexuality has gone off the rails and made her into someone warped. The most common example of the perverse adult is, of course, the homosexual. We likely have no better example of the ways in which people are thought to be defined by their sexuality than in the case of homosexuality. Some readers of this book will remember the t-shirts once common among homosexuals that defined "the homosexual life-style": doing laundry, going to work, cooking dinner. These t-shirts were precisely a response to the idea that a homosexual is defined solely by the character of their sexuality, that who they are is a matter of their sex. If this were true, it could not be simply a matter of their sexual activity, which was only one of many activities that they engaged in. It had, rather, to be a matter of their psychological makeup. A homosexual is homosexual not only in bed, but in all aspects of his or her life. That is what would make homosexuality perverse. And this is Foucault's point. For the homosexual, as for the other figures here, sexuality pervades character, defining it, making it what it is. Inasmuch as sexuality defines who we are, it is because our lives are expressions of our sexuality. When we discuss the figures of neoliberalism, I will argue that the normalization associated with sexuality no longer plays the role that Foucault saw it once playing. However, with regard to homosexuality we can see the remains of nineteenth- and early twentieth-century attitudes on full display, at least in certain quarters.

The Malthusian couple, unlike the previous three figures, is a figure of normality rather than abnormality. Foucault describes the Malthusian couple as the result of "an economic socialization via all the incitements and restrictions, the 'social' and fiscal measures brought to bear on the fertility of couples; a political socialization achieved through the 'responsibilization' of couples with regard to the social body as a whole. . . and a medical socialization carried out by attributing a pathogenic value—for the individual and the species—to birth-control practices."[14] The Malthusian couple is the goal of social practices that converged upon the couple: state practices of reproductive encouragement or discouragement, social service practices of monitoring and intervening on family sexual matters, medical practices of intervention into sexually oriented disorders, etc. This goal would be a stable familial couple with the proper number of kids and the proper expression—and repression—of the sexuality all of its members. It would be, in short, a normal family.

With the Malthusian couple we arrive at the animating idea behind much of Foucault's work during this period, that of normality and normalization. In *Discipline and Punish*, Foucault describes the sea change that takes place between what might be called pre-modern and modern forms of social constraint. In pre-modern forms, there is a binary distinction between the permitted and the forbidden. What was forbidden was mercilessly punished; everything else would be permitted. With the rise of modern society, technology, and social practices, this binary division gives way to what might be called a radiating space of normalization. In this space there is an ideal point—the normal—which exists at the center. We might think of the Malthusian couple as occupying this center. And, radiating out from it in all directions are various types and degrees of abnormality. The further one is from the center, the more abnormal one is. But, and this is just as important, this radiation is not linear. There is not simply a particular distance from the ideal point of the normal. Rather, there are all kinds of ways to radiate out from the center, that is, all kinds of ways to be abnormal. And if there are all kinds of ways to be abnormal, that entails two things. First, almost everyone is abnormal in one way or another. Second, and following from this, almost everyone is the legitimate object of social intervention, of practices designed to make one more normal.

The larger operation at play here, one that encompasses Foucault's discussions of discipline in *Discipline and Punish* and the apparatus of sexuality in the first volume of *The History of Sexuality*, is what has come to be called *normalization*. In his discussion of the prisons and the use of discipline within them, Foucault says, "The perpetual penality that traverses all points and supervises every instant in the disciplinary institutions compares, differentiates, hierarchizes, homogenizes, excludes. In short, it *normalizes*."[15] Normalization is the comparison of abnormalities against a posited norm, a comparison which justifies treatment of those abnormalities for the sake of bringing them closer to the norm. For instance, if the norm in sexuality is the Malthusian couple, then everyone who does not exist at the norm can be the object of psychological, social service, medical, psychiatric, or even judicial and police intervention. The goal of all this intervention, even if unachievable, would be the creation of another Malthusian couple. (And the unachievability of the goal itself acts to justify further intervention.) Because almost everyone is, in one way or another, distant from the norm, then everyone is legitimately subject to such intervention.

In *Discipline and Punish*, the image Foucault uses of this constant surveillance and interference is that of the "carceral archipelago."[16] The carceral archipelago, an image which echoes Aleksandr Solzhenitsyn's discussion of the Soviet Union's "gulag archipelago," consists of the various institutions that surveil and follow any perceived or even possible abnormality in order to be able to insert themselves into the lives of people in the name of greater normality. These are not only the penal institutions, but in addition (and, in Foucault's view, historically stemming from those institutions) social work agencies, personnel management, the proliferation of therapists and counselors, self-help books, academic social sciences such as psychology and sociology, etc. The carceral archipelago becomes co-extensive with society itself, overseeing behavior and always ready to step in and lend a normalizing hand.

Foucault does not argue, although he is sometimes taken to do so, that normalization is the only power operating in modern society. In fact, he says, "The power of the Norm appears through the disciplines. Is this the new law of modern society? Let us say rather that, since the eighteenth century, it has joined other powers—the Law, the Word (*Parole*), and the Text, Tradition—imposing new delimitations upon them." [17] Normalization is a recent form of the operation of power, one that is made possible by the availability of increasing technologies that permit surveillance and intervention, by the rise of the social sciences (which it also makes possible), and by the emergence of capitalism, for which the normal is a more useful category than the permitted since it is better aligned with productive efficiency. The rise of normalization does not overtake other forms of power, but instead is integrated with them, altering them and modifying itself in order to operate alongside them.

What is significant for our purposes here is twofold. First, the figures to which we have drawn attention here are characteristic of the pre-neoliberal period. They offer a contrast to the figures of the consumer and the entrepreneur. Second, the reason for this is that the more recent figures are not indebted to the larger project of normalization. This is a point to which we will return below when we discuss those figures themselves. Before doing so, I would like to offer a historical speculation that may tie together the figures and the political character of the pre-neoliberal period. This speculation is not central to our concerns here, which are centered on understanding the figures of neoliberalism. However, if correct, it would help explain the persistence of these figures as well as their partial demise during the more recent period.

The suggestion is this: the project of normalization is particularly consonant with the goals of what we might call *welfare-state capitalism*, Keynesian capitalism of the middle two-thirds of the twentieth century. In offering this suggestion, I need to hedge at the outset. As we have seen, in Foucault's view normalization does not arise in the twentieth century, but begins to emerge two centuries before, with the rise of capitalism. Welfare-state capitalism does not initiate normalization, nor does it generate its figures. My claim is more modest. It is that welfare-state capitalism is particularly suited to the project of normalization. It is especially amenable to a normalizing orientation.

Why is this? Welfare-state capitalism, in contrast to neoliberalism, does not see the individual on his or her own, exercising freedom in the marketplace in search of the best advantage. As we have seen, welfare-state capitalism sees a larger role for government intervention into the economy. In Keynes' view, this intervention is an economic one, performed with an eye toward increasing demand. However, the programs enacted during the period of welfare-state capitalism have a wider purview than just an economic one. The Roosevelt administration's creation of Social Security was followed by a more general welfarist orientation that led to the creation of Aid to Dependent Families, Food Stamps, various programs for the mentally handicapped and disturbed, anti-poverty initiatives, and Social Security Disability, to list just a few. Each of these required staff not only to distribute goods but also to monitor who was receiving those goods, assessing need and eligibility and also potential to be integrated into the mainstream economic order. That potential could be tapped through training programs and lower level jobs creation. In short, this welfarist orientation generated an entire apparatus of practices whose goal was the normalization of marginal populations. This normalization is in keeping with at least a broad interpretation of the Keynesian mandate that governments need to intervene in order to preserve economic health, a mandate that is rejected in its entirety by neoliberal theory and practice.

An example of the intimacy of normalization and welfare-state capitalism is offered by Foucault's colleague François Ewald in *L'Etat Providence*, a history of welfare-state practices in France. He seeks to show how, particularly over the course of the late nineteenth and early twentieth centuries, responsibility for social health evolved from private charity into a public duty, "the proliferation of insurance institutions and the birth of Social Security, the appearance of the welfare-state, one of the processes of socialization that characterize the contemporary history of our societies: *the socialization of responsibilities.*"[18] Roughly, during the nineteenth century, accidents, particularly worker accidents, were thought of as the responsibility of the worker. Over the course of the late nineteenth and early twentieth centuries, however, there was a shift. Accidents were no longer considered matters of individual responsibility. They were, instead, thought to be inevitable. This change corresponds to the rise of statistical and probabilistic thinking. Given certain working conditions, it was likely that x number of accidents would occur during y period of time. When and to whom those accidents would occur could not be predicted. But the overall probability of their occurring could. In this thinking, accidents were no longer individualized to those to whom they occur. They were socialized into a metric of *risk*. It is in this change that we can see both the rise of insurance (against risk) and "the socialization of responsibilities."

However, there is more to the story. "Risk serves not only to assess dangers, to locate or to localize them; it is at the same time, in the same gesture, a moral category: starting from which society prescribes to its members what can and cannot be done, behavior that is profitable to all and to each, as well as conduct that is harmful because it is socially costly."[19] Risk, then, does not simply shift responsibility to the social body. At the same time, it allows the social body to intervene upon the individual in order to lower the general incidence of risk. It creates social solidarity both from above and from below. From above, the individual's vulnerability is underwritten by the social institutions. From below, the individual is now bound to the social body through his or her obligation to act responsibly toward the social body. "The project of Social Security [by which Ewald means the entire apparatus of social guarantees, not simply the particular program for the elderly as in the US] is no longer solely that of covering individual risk, of guaranteeing a minimal security for individuals, of freeing them from need, Social Security wants to be and is a new practice of the *social contract*: Social Security is the institution across which is realized this contract of solidarity which constitutes the veritable relationship between individuals in society."[20]

This depiction of the welfare state is in keeping with the rise of the figures Foucault describes. Once again, we should bear in mind that these figures emerge over the course of several centuries. However, the rise of the sexualization of humanity takes a leap forward with the emergence of psychoanalysis early in the twentieth century, a leap that corresponds chronologically and psychologically with the socialization of risk that Ewald describes. Moreover, the interventions into individual behavior and the project of normalization generally are of a piece with the welfare state. If, in return for being insured by the state, individuals are asked to conform to the most efficient or least dangerous forms of behavior, then classifications of and interventions into perceived deviancy are not only warranted: they are obligatory. A society of solidarity around risk is a society in which each of the members has a duty to cleave to the proper social norm. The Malthusian couple is the ideal figure of that norm, and the other figures he describes are deviations from it. Those deviations must be intervened upon by the same social institutions that offer support for individuals: social services, medical personnel, the legal system, personnel officers, psychologists and psychiatrists. Social solidarity, in its concept and in its institutions, is inseparable from an individualized and individualizing social policing.

What happens, then, when we shift from a society of solidarity, a welfarist society, to a neoliberal one? In asking this question, we must be careful not to ascribe too radical a shift. There has been no wholesale jettisoning of the welfare state for a neoliberal one, or of normalization for something else. Nor have the figures of the past several centuries simply disappeared in favor of new ones. The shift is rather one of emphasis or dominance. As Foucault reminds us, several regimes of power often co-exist at the same time. What we are witnessing is not a radical break, but instead a passage from the dominance of one set of power relations to another. This passage characterizes all levels of society, from that of the state to relations among individuals. Our concern is primarily with the latter, and thus with the new figures that arise in the wake of the emergence of neoliberalism.

NOTES

1. Foucault, Michel, *The History of Sexuality, Vol. 1: An Introduction*. tr. Robert Hurley (New York: Random House, 1980 [1978]), p. 105.

2. Weber, Max, "'Objectivity' in Social Science and Social Policy," in Weber, Max, The Methodology of the Social Sciences. Ed. Edward A. Shils and Henry A. Finch. New York: Free Press, 1949, p. 90.

3. Weber, "'Objectivity' in Social Science and Social Policy," p. 90.

4. Weber, "'Objectivity in Social Science and Social Policy," p. 93.

5. Weber, "'Objectivity in Social Science and Social Policy," pp. 91–92.

6. Foucault, Michel, *Discipline and Punish: The Birth of the Prison*, Tr. Alan Sheridan (New York: Random House, 1977 [1975]), p. 277.

7. *Discipline and Punish*, p. 280.

8. Foucault, Michel, "So is it important to think?" In J. Faubion (ed.), tr. Robert Hurley and others. *Power The Essential Works of Michel Foucault 1954–1984. Volume Three* (New York: New Press, 2000), p. 458.

9. *The History of Sexuality, Vol. 1*, p. 104.

10. *The History of Sexuality, Vol. 1*, p. 157.

11. *The History of Sexuality, Vol. 1*, p. 21.

12. *The History of Sexuality, Vol. 1*, p. 104.

13. Foucault, Michel, *Abnormal: Lectures at the Collège de France 1974-1975*, tr. Graham Burchell (New York: Picador, 2003 [1999]), pp. 245–6.

14. *The History of Sexuality, Vol. 1*, pp. 104–5.

15. *Discipline and Punish*, p. 183.

16. *Discipline and Punish*, p. 297.

17. *Discipline and Punish*, p. 184.

18. Ewald, François, *L'Etat Providence* (Paris: Bernard Grasset, 1986), p. 10.

19. *L'Etat Providence*, p. 384.

20. *L'Etat Providence*, p. 403.

THREE

The Figures of Neoliberalism: Consumer and Entrepreneur

The economic shifts we canvassed earlier could not have been accomplished without the complicity of various governments. To describe neoliberalism solely in terms of the withdrawal of the state from social life, then, would be a mistake. At the level of the state, the question is not only what states no longer did (fostering social solidarity, supporting the intervention into individual behavior), but also what they were doing instead. Foucault describes this new form of behavior in terms of ensuring the smooth working of the market. In his view, what distinguishes neoliberalism (and its German and Austrian predecessor, ordoliberalism) from the classical liberal thought associated with people like Adam Smith is a loss of the belief that markets will emerge and thrive naturally. For neoliberals, governments are required in order to ensure that markets don't go off the rails. Rather than intervening in markets, as Keynes would prescribe under certain conditions, governments must instead frame the economic sphere in such a way as to allow the proper operation of markets. "Government must not form a counterpoint of a screen, as it were, between society and economic processes. . . Basically, it has to intervene on society so that competitive mechanisms can play a regulatory role at every moment and every point in society and by intervening in this way its objective will become possible, that is to say, a general regulation of society by the market."[1]

This framing, however, is far less intrusive on an individual level than the normalization characteristic of the welfare state. It does not seek to make individuals conform to particular social roles, but instead leaves them to participate in the economic sphere as they see fit (or as they are fit to participate). This makes the relationship between individuals and the economy more intimate, more direct. For instance, rather than being subject to psychological intervention in order to normalize one's relationship to one's job and one's place in society, one is left instead to find one's way in an economic world whose influences will be characterized not by normalization but by the dictates of the market. It is not surprising, under these circumstances, that the figures of neoliberalism have a more economic hue. To gesture at this shift, we might say that the issue for individuals is no longer whether they are normal, but whether they are participants in the market, whether they are in or out. And, since market rationality is central to neoliberalism, the market becomes spread across our lives. Not only our economic but also our political, social, and personal relationships all become markets, and we better and worse participants in those markets.

Before turning to the two-fold character of that participation, we should perhaps pause for a moment over a recent phenomenon that might seem to constitute a return to normalization. That is the rise, in the wake of fears over terrorism, of increased surveillance. One is screened at airports, given background checks when applying for jobs, viewed by cameras when walking around central London. Moreover, we surveil one another ceaselessly with our camera phones. Aren't these apparatuses of observation just the kind of thing Foucault describes as central to normalization? Don't they constitute the return of what he calls in *Discipline and Punish* "panopticism?"

This is a large and difficult issue, but we should address at least two remarks to it. First, the increase in surveillance is not part of neoliberalism. Although it may help ensure the smooth operation of markets—by, for instance, suppressing social disturbance or keeping attention focused on the threatening Other rather than on the injustices of the market—it is not directly a part of the neoliberal order. But this does not mean that it is a return to normalization. I believe the matter is more complex than that, although I can only gesture at that complexity here. On the one hand, one might say that knowing that one is observed will make one more cognizant of and careful about one's behavior. In fact, as Foucault points out, one doesn't have to be observed in order to do so; there only has to be the constant threat of observation. As he notes about Jeremy Bentham's proposed Panopticon, there doesn't have to be anyone observing from the central tower of the prison complex. It only has to be the case that the central tower, which cannot be seen into by prisoners, *might* have someone in it in order for the prisoners to act as though they were always being observed. "Hence the major effect of the Panopticon: to induce in the inmate a state of consciousness and permanent visibility that assures the auto-functioning of power."[2] The ubiquity of surveillance might seem then to be pressing us towards normalization.

On the other hand, the various other institutions and practices that composed normalization have atrophied. If people are observed, this is not in order to make them into Malthusian couples. They are not being intervened upon for the purpose of normalizing them. If they are intervened upon, it is only to incarcerate them. Constant surveillance in the current period is not combined with the kinds of practices that would make it normalizing in the ways that that happened over the course of the previous century. There are certain behaviors that are less likely to occur, but those are only behaviors that would get one recognized as a threat to the state or the market.

Moreover, there is a certain way in which the ubiquity of surveillance and observation may even work *against* normalization. If one is always in front of a camera, one gets used to displaying oneself, warts and all. In fact, if one is to be noticed, it might behoove one to flaunt one's eccentricities. We see this occurring, for instance, in the current popularity of Facebook, where people seek to stand out not by hiding their differences from the normal but by accentuating them. A neoliberal society into which constant surveillance is introduced, then, may become less a society of normalization (except at the margins) and more a society of display.

Turning, then, to the figures of neoliberalism, we can separate them if we recognize that our participation in the market unfolds in at least two ways. As we will see, these two ways are not exclusive. They are distinct, but are often intertwined. These ways of participating give rise to two figures, that of the consumer and the entrepreneur. I don't want to claim that the consumer and the entrepreneur are the only two figures of neoliberalism. There may well be others. Neoliberalism is a relatively recent phenomenon, and it's often difficult to see exactly what is at issue in a given time period until one has more distance from it. It is no accident, for instance, that most of Foucault's genealogical studies focus on events that happened over a hundred years ago, or that his only foray into post–World War II history is a single lecture series, *The Birth of Biopolitics* and its study of neoliberalism. One might want to argue that it is folly to seek to understand a historical period while one remains ensconced within it.

This, however, would be a step too far. It is one thing to admit the difficulty of comprehending one's historical situation "from the inside," one might say. (Although it is true to say that when one comprehends an earlier historical situation, it is still from within the context of one's own.) The heat of the historical moment, the emergence of trends that cannot be recognized as trends until later, the occurrence of events of which one is not aware: all of these place limitations on any attempt to understand the present moment. However, this does not mean that we must remain silent about it. There are things we can say with some confidence, others we can speculate about, and still others that arise for us as vague intuitions. We may be mistaken about any or all of these, but this should not deter us. After all, the history of science has shown that we can be mistaken about what appears to be obvious or well entrenched. The project of understanding our present moment "from within," then, is a project that, while fraught, need not be thought of as futile. We do our best to understand where we are because it is important that we do so. But we recognize that our best may yet lead us astray.

In that light, the two figures we are about to consider are not to be thought of as the exhaustive figural legacy of neoliberalism. It would not be at all surprising if, in historical retrospect, it emerged that there were indeed others, or that the ones offered here were not exactly as we will describe them. However, I believe that the depictions of the consumer and the entrepreneur offered here will resonate with readers, that readers will be able to see themselves and their world within them. And I hope that, with these depictions in hand, that world will appear with more clarity. And, to anticipate, to the extent to which the depictions of these figures is accurate, we will be able to see how it is that they can be resisted through forms of friendship as well as a solidarity that can emerge from or be modeled on friendship. And, from the other side, we will be able to see how these figures threaten friendship, and why therefore we must be aware of the insidious influence they can have upon our lives.

The first figure, that of the consumer, is perhaps the most obvious and the most often discussed. We all know the consumer. The consumer is not simply the person that buys things. Things have been bought for a long time without the figure of the consumer emerging from all this buying. Rather, the consumer is the figure for whom buying is a central part of the sense of who one is. One identifies oneself as a consumer, and embraces that identification either explicitly or tacitly. Before embarking on a more rigorous discussion of the consumer, let us look at a few surface manifestations of it.

First, there is the central role that the mall has played in the recent construction of social life. Where teenagers and young adults once gathered in public spaces—the street or the public square—there has been, over the course of the last thirty or forty years, a movement to the mall as the central space in which these groups socialize. (There is also, to some extent and for smaller groups, the congregation at fast food restaurants, which are like malls writ small.) Formerly, in the street, socialization would largely consist in games of various sorts, from bike riding to baseball and stickball to games of verbal skill (and abuse). By contrast, malls are rigorously policed and the activities within them restricted. There is little else to do but hang out and shop. As a result, inasmuch as malls are a central space of socialization, shopping becomes a central form of activity associated with socialization and in turn a central way in and through which one identifies oneself and one's relationships.

Moreover, with the rise of the mall as the central public space of socialization, interpersonal interaction becomes more homogenized. One hangs out with one's friends, or at most with others who shop. The possibility of meeting people with different ideas or lifestyles or economic statuses is nearly foreclosed. As Zygmunt Bauman, a social theorist who has reflected doggedly on the rise of consumerism, points out, "The main feature of 'public, but not civil' places. . . is the *redundancy of interaction*. If physical proximity—sharing a space—cannot be completely avoided, it can be perhaps stripped of the challenge of 'togetherness' it contains, with its standing invitation to meaningful encounter, dialogue and inter-action. If meeting strangers cannot be averted, one can at least try to avoid the dealings."[3]

More recently, virtual socialization through texting, instant messag-ing, and online live video has emerged alongside the mall as a dominant form of socialization. This does not place one in a context of shopping. Has this had, or will this have, the effect of diminishing the consumerist character of our lives? One cannot say for certain, but I suspect that the answer is that it will not. This is for two reasons. First, virtual socializa-tion (to which we will return briefly in the discussion of virtual friend-ship in the appendix), because it is virtual, cannot entirely replace face-to-face interaction. People still like to get together in the same space and time. Inasmuch as they do so, and inasmuch as they are young enough not to have their own private space, they have very few choices as to the venue for their interaction other than the mall. One may spend less time in physical proximity with one's friends, but the time one spends in such proximity is often spent at the mall. Second, just as socialization has, to some extent, gone virtual, so has shopping. The same computer or iphone with which I am in contact with my friends is the means by which I shop, look for places to shop, or in other ways consume entertainment.

And this latter is the second surface manifestation of the consumer. Many of us have come to look upon large aspects of our lives in terms of the consumption of entertainment. This is also a phenomenon of the vir-tual world: we amuse ourselves by surfacing the web, shopping, watch-ing YouTube or pornography or videos of missed television programs. Whatever it is that we do virtually, much of it is bound to the consump-tion of entertainment. This phenomenon seeps across our lives in ways that we do not often recognize. For instance, in my own experience as a professor I am recently often confronted by students who see their educa-tion as a matter of entertainment. They bring their laptops to class (well, not to my class, but that's only because I prohibit it), and will pay atten-tion when something that strikes their interest arises while otherwise checking their email or spending time online. There are, of course, vari-ous and as yet not entirely understood effects of this sort of multi-tasking. However, although many students might deny that they see their educa-tion as a form of entertainment, their behavior is consonant with an inter-pretation of them along those lines.

One might want to object that it is not the rise of online communica-tion that has initiated this turn, but in fact the pre-neoliberal rise of television. There is no reason to doubt that television has had the effect of moving people toward a passive consumption of entertainment. Moreover, in some very minimal way online consumption requires a less passive engagement with the medium of entertainment. However, the ubiquity of virtual communication in our lives has ramified the effect of televisions—which, after all, was until recently an appliance one had to situate oneself at home in order to consume—so that entertainment is not something we go to, but rather something that follows us around.

A third surface manifestation of the consumer is branding. Branding happens in at least two ways, the second of which is more deeply entwined with the figure of the consumer, although it is related to the first, which is that of ubiquitous advertising. The Fedex Orange Bowl, Enron Stadium, the Sprint Halftime Report, the Aflac trivia question, to pick a few sports examples, display the inescapability of corporate branding in navigating one's world. It is difficult to enter a public space without being confronted with a corporate name or logo that has attached itself to anything from a building to a bathroom stall. In her earlier book, *No Logo*, Naomi Klein discusses the character (and structure) of a world pervaded by branding. She explains, "The effect, if not always the original intent, of advanced branding is to nudge the hosting culture into the background and make the brand the star. It is not to sponsor culture but to *be* the culture."[4]

When corporate branding is taken up by consumers who in turn identify with corporate brands, then another form of branding takes hold, one in which the consumer brands himself or herself. We can see this phenomenon particularly in clothing, although it appears elsewhere. Whether it is Nike shoes, Ralph Lauren polo shirts, Rainbow sandals, or some other form of wear, people—particularly teenagers, but increasingly pre-teens—are concerned about clothing designers in a way they had not been a generation previous. Speaking personally, I am surprised at the difference between my kids' relation to clothing and my own. I don't think I ever knew the brands of what I wore. For my kids, it is imperative to know what the designer is, and different social groups are often distinguished not simply by the types of clothes they wear, but by the designer of those clothes. This phenomenon was captured in a thematically horrific way in 1991 with Brett Easton Ellis' *American Psycho*. However, the branding he mocked then has continued and even expanded over the last two decades.

The rise of the mall as the central public space of socialization, the infiltration of entertainment into all aspects of our lives, and the preponderance of branding are all expressions of the emergence of the figure of the consumer. We are not saying, of course, that people were not consumers in some fashion before the emergence of neoliberalism. People have bought and consumed things from the beginning of trade economies. What is new is not the consumer, but the *figure* of the consumer, the creation of someone whose identity is deeply tied to their activity as a consumer. We might say, at the risk of oversimplification, that the difference between someone who consumes and the consumer as a figure is the difference between consumption as what one does and consumption as who one is. The oversimplification here would lie in thinking that who one is as a figure of the consumer is exhaustive of one's identity. As we will see, the figure of the consumer does not preclude the figure of the entrepreneur. Nor will it exclude the possibility of friendship, which can cut against both of these figures. Just as Foucault's figures of the masturbating child, the hysterical woman, or the perverse adult did not exhaust the identity of those who were created as a result of sexual practices, so the consumer as a product of neoliberalism, while much more deeply a consumer than in previous periods, is not all that one is.

What, then, is the figure of the consumer? We can identify the figure as embodying three themes: consumption as opposed to creation or production, inhabiting a time frame of the present, and individualization in a particular way. Let us look at each in turn.

Zygmunt Bauman contrasts the consumer society with the previous producer society (roughly, the society during the period of industrial production) this way. "[C]onsumerism is an attribute of society. For a society to acquire that attribute the thoroughly individual capacity for wanting, desiring and longing need to be, just as labour capacity was in the producers' society, detached ('alienated') from individuals and recycled/reified into an extraneous force which sets the 'society of consumers' in motion and keeps it on course as a specific form of human togetherness, while by the same token setting specific parameters for effective individual life strategies and otherwise manipulating the probabilities of individual choices and conduct."[5] There are several aspect of this passage to note, first of all the contrast between production and consumption. During the period of industrial capitalism, people identified themselves largely as producers. They were consumers, but their sense of themselves lay more in their role as producers than as consumers. This is not surprising, since consumer goods were more limited and scarce, and advertising not as pervasive as it has become. More recently, and especially with the rise of neoliberalism, people have begun to identify less with what they produce and more with what they consume. The brief examples we canvassed offer some cursory evidence of this.

I believe that the distinction between producing and consuming captures something important about the changes in how we identify ourselves, but there is more to it than that. To see what this "more" is, we can contrast two types of games children have played: stickball and video games. Stickball, a game played much more often before the rise of neoliberalism, is like baseball, but played with a stick (often a broomstick) and a light rubber ball. Bases are made up of whatever appears usable for such in the environment. Playing stickball involves the use of certain imaginative capacities. One has to consider one's environment in terms of a baseball field, and one's household items (ex. a broom) in terms of baseball equipment. Then one arranges the environment and plays the game, which is a physically active one. By contrast, video games are already set up. (They are more like the old board games in that way.) One does not actively imagine, manipulate, or physically navigate one's environment. One plays a games whose structure has been designed, down to the last detail, by others.

This contrast is not one between producing and consuming, strictly speaking. It is more exactly a contrast between creation and consumption. In this case, what is created—the stickball game—does not result in the appearance of some new item in the same way we would think of industrial production resulting in the appearance of a good. On the other side, the consumption of a video game is not consumption in the sense of buying, but rather in the sense of being entertained rather than entertaining oneself. Beneath the distinction Bauman marks between production and consumption is the distinction between creation and consumption, of which Bauman's distinction is an important subset. The difference I want to mark with the latter distinction is one between the active involvement in a creative engagement with one's environment and the more passive consumption of goods that are already there. This consumption is *more* passive rather than *completely* passive, since video games are, to one degree or another, interactive, in contrast for instance to television viewing.

In marking this contrast, we do not want to romanticize previous forms of play over current ones. Both television and cinema, which are forms of more passive consumption, pre-date the rise of neoliberalism. (Although cinema is a more complex case, at its best involving the viewer in a web of emotional and intellectual engagements, much like reading good literature.) However, the dominance of passive consumption over active creation is a central element of consumerism, and is instantiated in the figure of the consumer. That is to say, inasmuch as we are consumers our lives and at least implicit sense of ourselves is bound to consumption as an activity of more or less passive incorporation of our environment rather than actively engaging it in a creative fashion.

Bauman's definition of consumerism contains other themes as well, but they are, with one exception, bound up with the figure of the consumer. His reference to "setting specific parameters for effective individual life strategies," for instance, can be read as an alternative articulation of the concept of a figure. And the claim that consumerism instantiates a new form of "human togetherness" is consonant with the idea that we relate to one another as consumers, an idea that we be discussed at length in the following part of the book. The one exception is the claim that these life strategies involve "manipulating" individual choices. This is not a matter solely of describing the figure of the consumer, but instead of accounting for it through social practices. It may sound a bit conspiratorial, as though those involved in capitalist production seek to create the figure of the consumer in order to sell goods. In fact, Benjamin Barber sounds this theme when he writes that, "Today, [capitalism's] productive capacity has outrun the needs it once served even as its distributive capacity has been stymied by the growing global inequalities it has catalyzed. Depending for its success on consumerism rather that productivity, it has generated an ethos of infantilization that prizes the very attributes the Protestant ethos condemned."[6] (We will return to Barber's theme of infantilization in a moment.) However, we need not interpret Bauman's claim as a conspiratorial one. Instead, the idea can be that in the course of neoliberalism's rise, and with it the concomitant rise of the figure of the consumer, individual choices have become funneled toward available consumer goods rather than other activities that might constitute other kinds of selves.

Aligned with consumption over creation and production, the time frame of the figure of the consumer is the present. This is not difficult to see. The consumer is engaged with his or her current consumption rather than with the future or the past. What has happened is of no particular interest, because it has no relation to the current moment of entertainment. Neither is what will happen of interest, because it likewise has no bearing on the current moment, and moreover requires the active envisioning of a time that is not yet, an envisioning that conflicts with the passivity of consumption.

There may seem to be an ironic convergence here between the figure of the consumer and those philosophies, like Buddhism or Stoicism, that counsel living in the moment. And indeed the consumer does live in the moment. However, this living contrasts sharply with Buddhist or Stoic recommendations. For them, to live in the present means to inhabit it fully, to be actively engaged with it. The consumer does not actively engage with the present, but instead incorporates it, asks of it the provision of pleasure or entertainment. We might say that these philosophies require their followers to throw themselves into the present, where the consumer demands of the present that it throw itself at him or her.

In thinking about the inhabiting of the present, Bauman again provides assistance through two helpful references. "As lived by its members, time in the liquid modern society is neither cyclical nor linear, as it used to be for the members of other known societies. It is, instead, to use Michel Maffesoli's metaphor, *pointillist*—or, to deploy Nicole Aubert's almost synonymous term, *punctuated* time. . . Pointillist time is broken up, or even pulverized, into a multitude of 'eternal instants'. . . self-enclosed monads, separate morsels, each morsel reduced to a point ever more closely approximating its geometric ideal of non-dimensionality."[7] We should probably distance ourselves from the idea that the eternal instants of consumerism shrink to a point of non-dimensionality. That seems to go a bit far. The present of consumer time is not, or at least often not, a diminishing instant. But it is a now, and in an important way a series of nows. In that sense, consumerist time is pointillist.

The consumer is not concerned with either the past or the future, but with what is happening to or in front of him or her at the present moment. To shop, for instance, is to be concerned with what one is buying now, how it looks or feels or how it can entertain. There is a certain eroticism to this kind of shopping that makes it like sex. One is caught up in the moment of consumption. What is of primary concern are the sights, sounds, smells, and tactile sensations in which one is immersed. The future and the past do not matter at these moments. What is true of this form of shopping is also true of being entertained at the movies or in front of one's computer screen. If the entertainment is working, it is because it is absorbing, it takes on one as one takes it in. One does not participate in the creation of this absorption, to be sure, but one is unfolded within it.

There might be some hesitation to accept the idea that the consumer is entirely focused on the present. While the past is likely of little concern, doesn't the future play a role for the consumer? For example, doesn't one shop in order to wear or listen to or play something in the future? Undoubtedly this is the case, but for the figure of the consumer this future's bearing on the act of consumption is a minimal one. Of course, one may say to oneself, "It's okay to buy this, because I'll need it for x or y or z occasion." But that is only an excuse. It is the permission slip one writes for oneself in order to be able to buy the item that is, at this moment, beckoning. The future, when it is brought to consciousness, is largely if not entirely a support for the present of a consumption. What matters is how I am feeling now, as I buy or watch or play or listen to this particular item in front of me.

This is why consumer time is pointillist. It is not that the "eternal instants" shrink into non-dimensionality. It is rather that each instant is unconnected, or at least not deeply connected, to the others. Again the analogy with sex is apt. To have sex is not to do so once and for all. The urge rises periodically, and the previous act of sex will not satisfy the future urge. That has to be satisfied in its moment. Likewise, the act of buying this coat or watching this video lasts only as long as the consumption. Then one must move on to the next consumptive moment. This is what Richard Layard and others have termed the "hedonic treadmill."[8] One has to keep moving from this moment of pleasure or enjoyment to the next, because no the satisfactions of consumerism do not last much past the boundaries of the consuming act. In contrast to sex, there isn't even an afterglow worth remarking on.

Robert Lane, a sociologist to whose work we will return in the next part of this book, has detailed the ways in which what he calls "materialism" and what we are calling consumerism create unhappiness, and thus reinforces consumer activity and, as we are arguing here, the creation of the figure of the consumer. In *The Loss of Happiness in Market Democracies*, he argues that "Materialists tend to be less happy than others (1) because something about their values and practices is unsatisfying; or (2) because the kinds of people who choose materialist values carry within them the seeds of unhappiness. Both hypotheses are plausible."[9] Lane details how the reliance on extrinsic rather than intrinsic rewards, the loss of self-determination, and the desire for material goods often lead to or reinforce unhappiness. However, rather than motivating people to reject materialism, people are continually reinserted into it, through "socialization, market experience of contingent reinforcement (plus ideology), and evolutionary theory. They are interrelated: the relative importance of socialization depends on what the market teaches everyone in market societies, which, in turn, depends on the nature of human kind — evolutionary theory."[10] Lane is not arguing here that it is human nature that creates materialism or consumerism. Rather, human nature in the form of a general acquisitiveness is taken up and molded by contemporary market societies in ways that creation materialism and its consequent unhappiness. Although Lane does not note this, socialization of this type is self-reinforcing. If one is socialized to consider consumerism to be meaningful, and yet one finds oneself unhappy, one will do what one knows in order to cure that unhappiness. That is to say, one will consume. Thus the hedonic treadmill.

It is because of the dominance of the present in contrast to past and future that Barber, in the quote cited above, can think of the consumer as infantilized. "The ethics of narcissism promote and reflect a preference for the timeless present over temporality itself — whether past or future. . . embodied in an infantilizing ethos, the liberation from time has become an obliviousness to history and a foolish ignorance of mortality."[11] Children are caught up in the present. They do not worry about the past, and are certainly not concerned with their mortality. We often marvel at kids, at their ability to inhabit the moment, make a game of whatever is around them, show little concern for what might await them down the road. This is also why advertising to children is restricted. Whatever they want, they want it now, without recognizing the limits of what can be bought and what effects buying it might have. It is this phenomenon that Barber cites when he argues that consumer capitalism, in its unending imperative to sell us goods we don't really need, infantilizes us. We are told that we deserve this item, that we have earned it, that everyone else has it or that no one else has it, that it is who we are or who we want to be. It makes us want this thing in front of us, now and not later.

If consumer capitalism infantilizes adults, however, it also creates consumers out of infants. Juliet Schor, who has studied the rising trend of turning children into consumers in *Born to Buy*, writes, "Kids and teens are now the epicenter of American consumer culture. They commend the attention, creativity, and dollars of advertisers. Their tastes drive market trends. Their opinions shape brand strategies. Yet few adults recognize the magnitude of this shift and its consequences for the futures of our children and our culture."[12] She details this shift and discusses the deleterious effect it has on children, for instance the association of a materialist orientation with lower self-esteem and higher anxiety. However, it is the phenomenon rather than its outcome that is relevant for us here. While Barber claims that consumerism infantilizes adults, Schor argues that consumerism prepares children to be consumers as adults. These findings do not contradict each other. Rightly viewed, they complement each other. But their complementarity is best understood through the lens of an orientation toward the present.

To infantilize an adult, to render them as a child, is to undercut their ability to self-reflect. It is to undermine their ability to step away from the immediacy of their situation and to ask probing questions about it. That is to say, it is to plunge them unreflectively into the present. Alternatively, to turn a child into a consumer is to blunt their development into self-reflective beings. It is to discourage wider considerations on who one is and what one wants to be, and to substitute for those considerations the imperative of present consumption. Benjamin's and Schor's studies converge on the idea that the consumer is, and is encouraged to be, a creature of the present moment. His or her current material desires, desires to have or to enjoy, should be shielded from considerations about past experience or future projects and focused solely on the time being.

Passive consumption and a focus on the present are two of the main characteristics of the figure of the consumer. The third is an individualized egoism. We can call this egoism "individualized" because it does not rest primarily on a group solidarity. Individualized egoism is distinct from, say, the egoism of a racial group that believes itself superior to a different racial group. There is an egoism that white racists have regarding blacks: they think they are superior to and therefore deserve more than blacks. They focus on their needs as opposed to the needs of blacks, but do so as a group. For each of them, insofar as they are racists, it is not *my* superiority or *my* needs that are privileged, but *ours*. This is one of the elements of racism that makes it so dangerous. The group solidarity it involves can easily be transformed into mob activity.

Consumerist egoism is not like that. It is focused on the individual consuming, concerned with his or her pleasure, enjoyment, or entertainment. This does not mean that the joys of consumerism cannot take place alongside others. It can, and often does. One plays video games with others, watches television or movies with others, shops with others, texts with others. Although navigating the Internet can be done by oneself, it does not have to be. There is a difference, however, between the group solidarity of being with others and a more individualized being alongside. In this difference, the consumer falls largely on the latter side. While there can be some sharing that occurs with the enjoyment associated with consumerism, it is largely an individualized phenomenon.

The individualized egoism of the consumer can be seen largely to derive the two previous characteristics. After all, if one is passively consuming what is in front of one in the present, one is naturally more oriented toward one's own consumption than toward that of others. Further, one can take the contribution of each of these characteristics in turn to see its contribution to the third one. Passivity, as opposed to creativity, is more nearly a solitary relation to the world. In passivity, the orientation toward the world is centripetal rather than centrifugal. The world moves toward one, offering its experiences for the consumption of the one whose activity is to appropriate or ingest them rather than to engage with them. In creative or productive activity, it is necessary to manipulate aspects of the world. That places that activity out in the world, where others are also engaged in forms of creative activity and in which a co-participation can evolve, if it does not already exist. By contrast, passivity would require those others to come toward one. And, inasmuch as those others are themselves consumers, that coming-toward is unlikely to happen.

The orientation toward the present also contributes to individualized egoism. The parameters of the present do not allow for, or at least encourage, reflection on the effects of one's current activity on others. Consequences for others occur later, not now. They do not concern the present moment and are therefore of limited, if any, relevance. If time is more or less pointillist in its unfolding, the horizons of the world become much more limited than they would be if one lived a richer or more full-blooded orientation toward time. As a result, others become difficult to see, their experiences or needs more difficult to recognize. As time narrows toward the present, one's vision narrows toward oneself.

Although passivity and pointillist character of time point toward an individualized egoism, they do not entail it. It is possible to be both passive and oriented toward the present without being a consumer. People who watch a film by the late Swedish director Ingmar Bergman will often experience the pain of one or another of its characters (a pain that Bergman makes unmistakable for anything else). This pain can be experienced passively and in the moment of the viewing. (One might object here that to experience pain requires the ability to empathize with others, and so is not wholly passive. But we should distinguish between what the experience requires—the capacity for empathy—and what the experience involves—a placing before the viewer of the subject of pain.) Empathy of this sort is not an example of individualized consumerism. The latter brings out another aspect of the figure of the consumer, an aspect we have had in front of us so proximately that it is easy to take for granted. The consumer is oriented toward enjoyment or pleasure, not sadness or pain. The consumer is not simply an individualized experience; he or she is an individualized egoist, wanting to enjoy the goods that are placed in front of him or her. The problem with films like Bergman's, for instance, is that "they are just too depressing."

To be a consumer is not only to be passive and oriented toward the present. It is also to be focused on the enjoyment that present is obliged to offer. If the present fails to offer such enjoyment, it is falling short of what one asks of it. If we are to round out our understanding of the figure of the consumer, then, we must make explicit the particular sensual or emotional character of that figure, which is a desire for one's own pleasure. Of course, one does not have to be a consumer in order to desire pleasure. Pleasure as a motivator of human beings has been a constant theme in the history of philosophy, as well as that of the more recent history of psychology. What makes the figure of the consumer such is not just that he or she is oriented toward pleasure, but the combination of that orientation with passivity and an immersion in the present. And moreover, what makes the consumer a figure of neoliberalism is not only that one consumes one's joys passively in the present, but that this character is a dominant one in our time. We do not just consume, but are encouraged to be consumers, to think of ourselves as consumers, and to regard our fellow human beings as consumers.

This, by the way, goes some distance toward explaining the sense that many folks have that there is a rising sense of entitlement, particularly among younger people. I have experience this in my own classes, where an increasing—but still very much minority—percentage of students feel entitled to a decent grade without putting in a significant effort. In a culture that emphasizes passive enjoyment, people are encouraged to see their world as owing them amusement rather than offering them opportunities for creation or participation. This encouragement, in turn, leads to a sense of entitlement, one that instills the idea that, for instance, education should be a form of entertainment rather than a rigorous involvement in intellectual pursuits. (This latter claim should not, however, be taken as a defense of boring lecturers, many of whom are displays of intellectual rigor mortis rather than rigor.)

The consumer is one figure of neoliberalism. The other is the entrepreneur. As with the consumer, let us begin with a few superficial sketches of the entrepreneur. And at the outset, we should emphasize that the entrepreneur, like the consumer, is not an entirely new figure. Approaching one's life in terms of calculative self-enhancement is probably as old as humanity. Literature is replete with characters who use one another for their own ends, who see others as means for personal gain. It is not the existence of entrepreneurial activity, but its dominance and its sedimentation into a particular figure, that has been the legacy of neoliberalism with regard to entrepreneurship.

One relatively recent exhibition of entrepreneurial activity is the phenomenon of networking. Networking is not simply the formation of a web of relationships for the purpose of social or vocational gain. It is the positive valuation of such an approach to human relationships, and the thought of oneself as a networker, that has arisen in the wake of neoliberalism. The term *networking* as a self-description of activity is not applied as a term of disparagement. People describe themselves without shame as engaged in networking, and look upon others who are good at it with admiration. To see others as resources to be tapped, and to form a web of relationships based on these resources, and moreover to see oneself as someone who does this and to value this as part of one's identity—of one's sense of who one is—is to be in the grip of neoliberal entrepreneurship in the course of one's relationships. The impact this has on those relationships will be discussed in the next part of this chapter. For the moment, we want only to call attention to its existence.

Another display of entrepreneurial activity, one whose structure we will return to, is that of investment itself, and in particular the unmooring of investment from production. Successful investment, that is investment which brings return, has been divorced from the productivity that investment is traditionally supposed to support. As we saw above, Zygmunt Bauman contrasts the figure of the consumer with that of the producer; where people once thought of themselves as making things, now they think of themselves and consuming them. However, there is as deep a contrast between the entrepreneur as investor and the producer as between consumer and producer. In a recent article in *The New Yorker*, John Cassidy delineates the economic changes regarding finance capital. "Since 1980, according to the Bureau of Labor Statistics, the number of people employed in finance, broadly defined, has shot up from roughly five million to more than seven and a half million. During the same period, the profitability of the financial sector has increased greatly relative to other industries. . . during a period in which American companies have created iPhones, Home Depot, and Lipitor, the best place to work has been in an industry that doesn't design, build, or sell a single tangible thing."[13] The idea of return as its own reward, investment severed from its social contribution, is an exhibition of entrepreneurship that is characteristic of the neoliberal figure of the entrepreneur.

How might we define the figure of the entrepreneur? The entrepreneur is the figure who thinks of himself or herself in terms of investing toward the future for the sake of particular returns. These returns are often, but as we will see not necessarily, returns of personal gain. What characterizes the entrepreneur is not the self-centeredness of the activity of investment (although, as we will also see, the activity is individualized even when it is not self-interested), but its investment character. That character is in accordance with a particular type of economic rationality. Robert Lane sums up that rationality in "four parts: (1) the consistent, coherent (transitive) scheduling of preferences such that one has one's priorities right, (2) the development of a matrix of alternative means whereby to achieve each preferred goal, (3) assigning risks and probable payoffs in satisfaction for the ordered preferences, and (4) choosing accordingly."[14] We certainly do not want to claim that the figure of the entrepreneur rigorously follows this decision procedure. However, he or she does act in an informal way in accordance with it, particularly with the third part. The entrepreneur seeks the best return or payoff for a given investment of material or time.

In contrast to the figure of the consumer, that of the entrepreneur has a theoretical history, one that intersects with neoliberal history. Although we cannot offer a full treatment of that history here, it is worth gesturing at, in part because of its bond with neoliberal thought and practice. The figure of the entrepreneur arises in the heart of neoliberal economics, the Chicago School. In *The Shock Doctrine*, Klein argues that it is the theories of Milton Friedman, the most famous member of the Chicago School, that underlie the rise of neoliberalism. As she shows, it was his theories, and in fact his acolytes, that advised the Chilean government in 1973 after the overthrow of Salvador Allende, and in subsequent years were influential in Argentina, the Eastern bloc, and South Africa.

In sketching the rise of the entrepreneur in Chicago School thought, it would be instructive to start with one of its earliest figures, Henry Simons. This is as much because of what Simon left out of the neoliberal equation as what he put in. In a famous article from 1934, "A Positive Program for Lassez-Faire: Some Proposals for a Liberal Economic Policy," Simons articulates a broad defense of lassez-faire capitalism against the then-prevailing Keynesian policies of the New Deal. He argues that, "The real enemies of liberty in this country are the naïve advocates of managed economy or national planning."[15] That idea would remain central to the thought of Chicago School neoliberals up through the writings of Gary Becker and Milton Friedman. However, contrary to the orientation of these later thinkers, Simons does not believe that everything can be solved through market mechanisms, or that we should think of everything in market or entrepreneurial terms. He is, for instance, troubled by the profound inequalities of wealth distribution, and argues for a progressive income tax "based on the view (1) that reduction of inequality is per se immensely important; (2) that progressive taxation is both an effective means, and, within the existing framework of institutions, the only effective means to that end. . . "[16]

The entrepreneurial figure, or what Foucault calls *homo oeconomicus*[17], makes a fuller appearance in the 1950s to 1970s especially in the thought of Theodore Schulz and Gary Becker. Schulz introduces the concept of *human capital*, which claims that humans embody capital in a way that has been neglected by economists. For instance, a skilled worker has, through his skills, capital that can be invested in producing profit in a way that an unskilled worker does not. In other words, his or her skills can be thought of and even quantified as capital. This capital must be understood as such, and stands alongside more traditionally recognized forms of capital in any adequate assessment of the economic resources of a particular country or region. However, the concept of human capital has been neglected by traditional economics, which focuses solely on the latter forms of capital. As Schultz wrote in "Investment in Man: An Economic View" in 1959, "our knowledge about national wealth is almost wholly restricted to the non-human components, that is, to reproducible physical capital and land. The study of human wealth is everywhere neglected notwithstanding its importance and notwithstanding the fact that people all about us are investing in themselves."[18]

Schultz argues that we need to recognize the capital embodied in human beings in order both to understand how wealth is created and, inseparable from this, to be able to augment wealth, to invest resources in areas that will foster wealth creation. Of these, Schultz several times returns to investment in education as being a central example of the creation of human capital. In "Investment in Man," Schulz discusses both his own studies of money invested in education and Becker's analysis showing that "as of 1950, males were earning a 14.8 per cent return on what they had privately invested in acquiring their high school, college, and university education."[19] Later, in 1972, Schultz offers a quantitative discussion of rates of return on human capital for investments made at different levels: elementary school, high school, college, and graduate school.[20]

There are two aspects of the introduction of the concept of human capital that are worth recognizing. The first and most significant for our purposes is that it tends to think of human beings in terms of capital investment and return. Although this thought finds its fullest expression in the writings of Gary Becker, nevertheless the introduction of the concept of human capital is one that frames one's skills, knowledge, and perhaps even motivation in terms of capital that can be created by investment and in turn can be invested to create further return.

The other aspect of this view, particularly in Schultz's hands, is that it can have certain progressive implications. Neoliberalism as is currently practiced demands the withdrawal of public resources from the social service sector, of which education is a part. However, Schultz argues that public investment in education, especially elementary school education, actually creates wealth in the form of human capital. "Many poor countries are neglecting their elementary education relative to what they are spending on physical plants and equipment; moreover, the cost of this form of education is relatively low because of the opportunity costs of taking students at that age away from other useful work."[21] Schultz believes that, since humans embody capital, policies that increase that capital are more efficient at creating wealth, and that economists, by neglecting human capital, have neglected, as he puts it, "investment in man."

The central figure in the theoretical creation of the figure of the entre-preneur is undoubtedly Gary Becker. In Foucault's lectures on neoliberal-ism, he spends a number of pages discussing Becker's work, especially his approach to punishment. This is in part because of its contrast to the disciplinary apparatus characteristic of the welfare state. Rather than intervening at the level of the individual in a project of normalization, the model Becker promotes appeals to one's entrepreneurial instincts, regu-lating behavior by offering general social incentives and disincentives, for example creating punishments that act as opportunity costs across a pop-ulation for engaging in criminal activity. Foucault sums up this new model this way: "what appears on the horizon of this kind of analysis is not at all the ideal or the project of an exhaustively disciplinary society in which the legal network hemming in individuals is taken over and ex-tended internally by, let's say, normative mechanisms. . . we see instead the image, idea, or theme program of a society in which there is an opti-mization of systems of difference, in which the field is left open to fluctu-ating processes, in which minority individuals and practices are tolerat-ed, in which action is brought to bear on the rules of the game rather than on players, and finally in which there is an environmental type of inter-vention instead of the internal subjugation of individuals."[22]

For Becker, the entirety of human behavior can and should be under-stood on the model of investment and return. As he put it in his 1992 Nobel Prize lecture, entitled "The Economic Way of Looking at Life," "The analysis assumes that individuals maximize welfare *as they conceive it*, whether they be selfish, altruistic, loyal, spiteful, or masochistic."[23] Whether the question one faces is that of how much education to attain, whether to marry, how many children to have, whether to break the law, how to discourage discrimination against minorities, the best way to set-tle these questions, both at the level of personal decisions and at those of setting policy, is to look at the various types of return that can be ex-pected on the basis of different types of investment. "Human capital analysis starts with the assumption that individuals decide on their edu-cation, training, medical care, and other additions to knowledge and health by weighing the benefits and costs. Benefits include cultural and other non-monetary gains along with improvement in earnings and occu-pations, while costs usually depend mainly on the foregone value of the time spent on these investments."[24]

In keeping with this view, Becker has written on economic approaches to various phenomena, including not only punishment but discrimina-tion, family life, education, and employment. In each case, he offers a quantitative approach that balances the kinds of investments made with returns expected. For example, in "An Economic Analysis of Fertility," Becker argues that "Fertility is determined by income, child costs, knowl-edge, uncertainty, and tastes. An increase in income and a decline in price would increase the demand for children, although it is necessary to distinguish between the quantity and quality of children demanded. The quality of children is directly related to the amount spent on them."[25]

Central to the question of investment is that of the investment of time. In one of his most influential articles, "A Theory of the Allocation of Time," Becker argues that we allocate time in accordance with entrepreneurial considerations, seeking to maximize the return for a given amount of time deposited into an activity. One could, he argues, seek to maximize one's income by allowing the allocation of one's time "to be determined solely by the effect on income and not by an effect of utility. . . Households in richer countries do, however, forfeit money income for a greater amount of psychic income. For example, they might increase their leisure time, take a pleasant job in preference to a better-paying unpleasant one, employ unproductive nephews or eat more than is warranted by considerations of productivity."[26]

A striking example of how Becker's idea have suffused themselves into society arises in my own field of education. For Becker, schooling is primarily a matter of job training. "A school can be defined as an institution specializing in the production of training, as distinct from a firm that offers training in conjunction with the production of goods."[27] Going to school, like other activities, is an investment. One foregoes immediate employment in order to obtain skills that will bring greater remuneration later in life. As Becker puts the point, "schooling would steepen the age-earnings profile, mix together the income and capital accounts, introduce a negative relation between the permanent and current earnings of young persons, and (implicitly) provide for depreciation on its capital."[28] Although most current students in higher education don't think of their education in the precise terms Becker lays out, in the neoliberal period they are far more oriented toward the place of job training in higher education than students were a generation ago. In 1998, the *New York Times* reported that, "In the [annual UCLA] survey taken at the start of the fall semester, 74.9 percent of freshmen chose being well off as an essential goal and 40.8 percent chose developing a philosophy. In 1968, the numbers were reversed, with 40.8 percent selecting financial security and 82.5 percent citing the importance of developing a philosophy."[29]

One might get the impression that Becker's analyses are entirely oriented around personal gain. Although the entrepreneurial figure is, as we will argue, largely self-interested, self-interest is not necessary to Becker's thought. In his considerations on the investment of time and effort, the equations he creates allows for factoring in what he calls "altruism" as a motive for behavior.[30] One might ask, then, how one moves from Becker's thought, which, although entrepreneurial, seeks to incorporate altruism, to a neoliberal period in which such altruism or other-directedness is often thought to be at best inefficient and often naïve. Indeed, one might ask how the collective thought of Simon, Schultz, and Becker has been turned almost wholly toward self-interest.

Here the significant of Milton Friedman's thought assumes its role. In *The Shock Doctrine*, Naomi Klein argues that Friedman's ideas are centrally responsible for the rise of neoliberalism in the current period. Although, as we have seen, Friedman's ideas are woven in with those of others, especially in the Chicago School, and although one might say that there have been other developments (ex., the Arab Oil Crises of 1973) that have played an important role, it is undeniable that Friedman's influence stands above the others that we have sketched here in helping to shape the neoliberal period. And his ideas had no particular patience with altruism. This emerges particularly in his seminal 1970 article in the *New York Times*, "The Social Responsibility of Business Is to Increase its Profits."[31] There he argues that businesses do not have a responsibility to the wider community in which they operate, or what came later to be called the "stakeholders," but only to the stockholders or owners of those businesses. To act any other way would be a form of "taxation without representation," of utilizing the investment of stockholders for purposes they have not ratified. And, unless the stockholders explicitly say otherwise, the responsibility of businesses is to maximize profits. Or, as he says in *Capitalism and Freedom*, the reason the US has progressed over the past century is that, "The invisible hand [of the market] has been more potent for progress than the visible hand for retrogression."[32] What brings progress is not the action of governments or even individuals to assist others, but rather the unfettered operation of a market in which each individuals seeks to maximize her personal gain.

The picture we have sketched here of the entrepreneurial figure offers us an overview of what he or she looks like. We can turn at this point toward a delineation of the central elements of that figure. As with the consumer, the figure of the entrepreneur has three elements each of which merit discussion. In contrast to the passive consumption of the consumer, the entrepreneur is engaged in active investment. And in contrast to the temporal orientation toward the present of the consumer, the entrepreneur is oriented toward the future. However, in consonance with the consumer, the entrepreneur is an individualist figure, one that exists outside any configuration of social solidarity. This individualism displays a deep characteristic of neoliberalism, in ways we will need to investigate.

We can see the more active character of the entrepreneur in the descriptions given by Becker. The entrepreneur does not await entertainment, but instead seeks opportunity. In particular, he or she seeks opportunity for efficient investment of resources, of his or her human capital. This requires not both an assessment of one's contemporary context, its possibilities and limitations, and the active engagement with that context in order to yield the maximum return. It must be asked whether taking a job or going to graduate school will have the best net effect on one's future salary, and then one must act in accordance with the answer. It must be asked whether marrying this person will offer the best future or, instead, whether waiting for an unknown person to come along would make more sense, and then one must marry or wait. It must be asked whether schmoozing with this personage or that at one's professional conference might place one in a better position in one's field, and then the schmoozing must commence. Or, in a less self-centered vein, it must be asked whether putting one's child in this day school or that one will offer him or her better prospects for getting into a prestigious college, and then one must apply and, one hopes, send the child to the chosen school.

In approaching these decisions, the entrepreneur acts more or less in accordance with the model summarized by Robert Lane. One reflects upon and orders one's preferences, then develops a matrix of means for achieving them, then assigns payoffs for each possible course of action, and finally acts in accordance with the most efficient means to the best achievable ends. Of course, this coherence and precision of the approach Lane summarizes is rarely acting upon as explicitly as he has laid it out, although it does happen sometimes. More often, a general orientation toward efficiency and away from waste is the rule. However, the active creation of means toward ends rather than, as with the consumer, the more or less passive reception of the world, is the characteristic form of the entrepreneur's engagement with the world.

An amusing example (if not self-consciously so) of this type of behavior is offered by the judge Richard Posner in his account of the history of sex in *Sex and Reason*. Posner presents "a positive economic theory of sexuality, showing how the type and frequency of different sexual practices, as distinct from the sex drive and sexual preference (inclination, orientation) can be interpreted as rational responses to opportunities and constraints."[33] Among the benefits of sex are the procreation of children, the enjoyment of sexual activity, and the reinforcement of social bonds. Among the costs are those of finding a sexual mate, the expenses of raising children, and the sexual constraints of a particular culture. Posner believes that sexual behavior can be explained as the attempt to navigate the constraints in order to secure the benefits of sex most efficiently. All of this is rooted in Posner's sociobiological view of sexuality, one that sees men as seeking to procreate more children and women as seeking to retain men for material support in ensuring the development of their children (and thus the passing on of her genes). In the end, Posner offers an economic model for regulating sexuality, one that seeks to maximize the benefits and minimize the costs of such regulation. It includes a liberal view of abortion, disseminating public information about contraception, and limiting the role of government support for children born outside of marriage. This will foster the most efficient procreative strategies, given men's promiscuousness and women's protectiveness.

The activity of the entrepreneur should not be confused with productivity. The entrepreneur is not necessarily committed to creating anything, or at least anything of value. In this, the entrepreneur reflects the rise of finance capital that we noted earlier. Just as many of the derivatives traded on the market do not produce value, many of the investments the figure of the entrepreneur makes do not produce value. Time spent in networking that allows one to gain a better paying job, the development of a certain personal style in order to burnish one's image and thus garner social prestige, making an appearance at certain social events or securing invitations to those events for the sake of earning the admiration or envy of others: none of these produce value, but they are common ways in which we are encouraged to be entrepreneurial.

The time frame for the entrepreneur is not the present, as it is for the consumer, but the future. It is not what is happening now that matters, but what will happen if one follows this or that course of action. This follows from the means/end orientation of entrepreneurial activity. The entrepreneur is not content with the current context. This does not mean that she is unhappy with it. The entrepreneur may indeed find much to enjoy in the situation she inhabits. Being an entrepreneur does not preclude being a consumer, a point to which we will return. However, inasmuch as one is an entrepreneur, one must be dissatisfied with something in the current situation, dissatisfied enough to want to invest one's resources to change it: to develop a new contact, to have a child, to go to school. There must be something else one wants in addition to what one has, or at least something else one will want that will be unavailable unless one actively engages with the world. And so one acts with a view toward future reward.

To act toward the future is not entirely to neglect the present or the past. Of course, to be human is to be unable to remove oneself entirely from present and past, since humans have perception and memory. But even inasmuch as one is an entrepreneur, both temporal modes have bearing on who one is. The past is an inventory of lessons for future investment, a record of what has worked and what has not. The present offers the context that must be assessed for its potential benefits and liabilities. But both of these are folded into a vision of the future, of what is likely to happen depending on what course of action is chosen. The past and present are submitted to the future, even as the future has to answer to the guidance and constraints the former contain.

While contrasting with the consumer in being active and future-oriented, the neoliberal entrepreneur shares a deep bond with the consumer in having an individualist orientation, even an egoistic one. As we noted above, egoism is not a necessary characteristic of the entrepreneur as Becker conceives her. "All the implications derived for a single beneficiary continue to hold when there are many. In particular, an altruist internalizes all external effects of his actions on different beneficiaries as he maximizes the sum of his own income or consumption and the incomes or consumptions of his beneficiaries."[34] However, several factors have contributed to skewing the entrepreneur in a less altruistic direction. First, the theoretical domination of Friedman's thought has eclipsed altruistic considerations. His defense of personal and corporate gain has militated against weighing considerations of the general social good in deciding how best to invest one's resources.

Second, neoliberal economics have had their effect. As we have seen, neoliberal policies over the past thirty years have contributed to concentrating wealth among a few people at the expense of most others. Moreover, the withdrawal or retrenchment of public services in many countries has rendered people more vulnerable. Without a safety net, or even with a safety net that has developed holes in its netting, life becomes more precarious. Where wealth and support is less secure, people tend to look inward rather than outward. Their concerns begin to focus on themselves and their immediate dependents rather than on the general social welfare. Where the stakes are high and assistance is low, vision becomes more near-sighted. Neoliberal economics reinforces that near-sightedness by raising the level of individual insecurity. The political scientist Wendy Brown underlines this aspect of neoliberalism when she writes that, "In making the individual fully responsible for her- or himself, neoliberalism equates moral responsibility with rational action; it erases the discrepancy between economic and moral behavior by configuring morality as a matter of rational deliberation about costs, benefits, and consequences. But in doing so, it carries responsibility for the self to new heights: the rationally calculating individual bears full responsibility for the consequences of his or her action no matter how severe the constraints on this action—for example, lack of skills, education, and child care in a period of high unemployment and limited welfare benefits."[35]

Third, in the US an individualist orientation is consonant with long-standing American ideology. The individual who either pulls herself up by her bootstraps or overcomes the odds or utilizing her freedom to make something of herself: these are particularly American tropes, and they help cast the figure of the entrepreneur in an individualist direction. The entrepreneur is the one who, because of her wit and pluck, and by risking her economic, political, or social capital, emerges victorious in the venture upon which she embarks.

It is not an accident that it is individualism upon which both figures converge, in spite of their differences. This is partly because of the dominance of US culture around the world, and with it the dominance of individualism. It is also because it reinforces the reproduction of neoliberalism itself. As long as people are individualistically oriented rather than in solidarity, resistance against neoliberalism is likely to be muted. (We will return to this point in the last part of the book.) We have seen the effects of neoliberal economics, and it might give one pause as to why there is not been more opposition to its policies. There are, of course, many reasons for this. But one is that, inasmuch as people are being

created to be individualist consumers or entrepreneurs, the path to solidarity, and thus to resistance is at least partially blocked. The dominance
of individualism has hindered any collective movement of struggle
against the neoliberal order.

This contribution of neoliberalism to its own reproduction should not
be understood in conspiratorial terms. The elites have not gotten together
and decided to turn people in a more individualist direction in order to
blunt any opposition to neoliberal economics. Far from it. The elites are
as individualist as everyone else. As Foucault has insisted, rather than
thinking in terms of conspiracies we better understand the emergence of
political phenomena as the convergence of a variety of disparate factors.
In this case, the convergence of a dominance of neoliberal thought with a
historical opening for neoliberal practice, the creation of economic security that has resulted from that practice, the historical insistence of
American individualism combined with the current (if perhaps waning)
influence of American culture, the pervasiveness of advertising, and the
atrophy of the left in many economically advanced countries, have resulted in a reinforcement of an individualism that fits neatly with certain
orientations of the two figures we have discussed.

To this point, we have discussed these figures separately, as though
one could be either a consumer or an entrepreneurial figure, but not both.
And, in fact, there are differences between them. This does not require,
however, that a person cannot embody both the figure of the consumer
and the entrepreneur. In this, the figures of neoliberalism are like the
earlier figures Foucault describes. It is possible, for instance, to be both a
delinquent and a perverse adult, or a hysterical woman and yet someone
who is part of a more or less Malthusian couple. (Of course, it is not
possible to be a masturbating child and a perverse adult at the same time,
but not impossible to evolve from the former into the latter.) The point of
intersection between the two figures lies in the moment of the return on
investment, the profit which can be consumed. Inasmuch as one is an
investor, one aims toward profit, but is not interested in the consumption
of it. In fact, capitalist theory often counsels the re-investment of profit.
However, one can imagine profit, both monetary and non-monetary, that
would be consumed and, more significantly, that one would think of
oneself in terms of consuming.

Bauman provides an example of this in his tellingly titled *Liquid Love:
On the Frailty of Human Bonds.* "Objects of consumption serve the needs,
desires, or wishes of the consumer; so do children. Children are wanted
for the parental pleasures it is hoped they will bring. . . Having children
means weighing the welfare of another, weaker and dependent, being
against one's own comfort. The autonomy of one's own preferences is
bound to be compromised, and ever anew: year by year, daily."[36] Bauman is not arguing that everyone looks at children in these ways—in fact
he claims, as I will in the following chapters of this book, that there is

more to us and to our relationships than is created and fostered by neo-liberalism. Rather, he is arguing that we are encouraged to think of our relationships with children in these ways, as potential joys to be consumed resulting from investments we must make on the basis of cost-benefit analyses. This is in keeping with Becker's analyses of children, only with the focus on the consumption of pleasure rather than, as Becker puts it in some of his moods, the support one will later receive from children in one's dotage.

Other and less controversial examples abound. One invests time in professional relationships in order to secure a higher paying position, which in turn allows one to consume the monetary benefits of that position. Or one cultivates the company of prestigious people in one's field in order to bask in the attention they offer or the respect of one's less well-placed colleagues. Or one foregoes vacations in order to finance a child's education at an elite college in order to savor the vicarious success of the child (which does not preclude more altruistic concerns over the child's welfare). In all of these cases, while the entrepreneurial activity looks forward to generating a return, the consumerist activity occurs at the point of generation, where there is a good to be consumed.

It might be said that this intersection between consumer and entre-preneur is nothing other than a description of mundane human activity. We do things in order to reap rewards that we then consume. There is nothing particularly neoliberal about that. And this is certainly true. The consumption of rewards one has generated is coextensive with the history of the species. In that way, neoliberalism intersects with our common humanity. However, it is not merely the intersection that is at issue here. It is the character of the two streams that intersect. The particular character of the intersection of investment and consumption in neoliberalism is one that lays stress on the entrepreneurial and consumptive character of the streams. Inasmuch as one is subject to the neoliberal order, embody-ing its figures, one defines herself in the terms we have delineated here: activity with an eye to return, consumption with an eye to enjoyment. And if it is asked how else we might think of ourselves, we can offer two responses. The first is that it would be a measure of how deep the grip of neoliberalism is if it were hard to conceive our lives otherwise. The sec-ond would be to offer another way of thinking about ourselves. This other way will emerge over the course of the next chapter, as we investi-gate the possible character of our relationships with others, but within and against the legacy of neoliberalism.

NOTES

1. Foucault, Michel, *The Birth of Biopolitics: Lectures at the Collège de France, 1978–1979*, tr. Graham Burchell (New York: Palgrave Macmillan, 2008 [2004]), p. 145.
2. Foucault, *Discipline and Punish*, p. 200

3. Bauman, Zygmunt, *Liquid Modernity* (Cambridge: Polity Press, 2000), p. 105.

4. Klein, Naomi, *No Logo: Taking Aim at the Brand Bullies* (New York: Picador, 1999), p. 30.

5. Bauman, Zygmunt, *Consuming Life* (Cambridge: Polity Press), p. 28.

6. Barber, Benjamin, *Con$umed: How Markets Corrupt Children, Infantilize Adults, and Swallow Citizens Whole* (New York: W.W. Norton, 2007), pp. 36–37.

7. Bauman, *Consuming Life*, p. 32.

8. Layard, Richard, *Happiness: Lessons from a New Science* (New York: Penguin Press, 2005), p. 48.

9. Lane, Robert E., *The Loss of Happiness in Market Democracies* (New Haven: Yale University Press, 2000), p. 146.

10. Lane, *The Loss of Happiness*, p. 149.

11. Barber, *Con$umed*, p. 108.

12. Schor, Juliet B., *Born to Buy: The Commercialized Child and the New Consumer Culture* (New York: Scribner, 2004), p. 9.

13. Cassidy, John, "What Good is Wall Street?" *The New Yorker*, November 29, 2010, p. 51.

14. Lane, Robert E., *The Market Experience* (Cambridge: Cambridge University Press, 1991), p. 43.

15. Simons, Henry, "A Positive Program for Lassez Faire: Some Proposals for a Liberal Economic Policy," in Simons, Henry, *Economic Policy for a Free Society* (Chicago: University of Chicago Press, 1948), p. 41.

16. Simons, "A Positive Program for Laissez Faire," p. 65. In this passage he continues, "(3) that, in a world of competitive, invidious consumption, the gains at the bottom of the income scale can be realized without significant loss to persons of large income, so long as their rank in the income scale is unchanged; and (4) that drastic reduction of inequality through taxation is attainable without much loss of efficiency in the system and without much impairing the attractiveness of the economic game."

17. Cf. Foucault, *The Birth of Biopolitics*, esp. chap. 11.

18. Schultz, Theodore, "Investment in Man: An Economic View," *The Social Service Review*, Vol. 33, No. 2, June 1959, p. 110.

19. Schultz, "Investment in Man," p. 116.

20. Schultz, Theodore, *Human Resources* (New York: National Bureau of Economic Research, 1972), esp. pp. 28–34.

21. Schultz, "Investment in Man," p. 116. Later, in Human Resources, Schultz argues that elementary education offers a much higher rate of return than upper levels of education, even though the latter receive an inordinate amount of public funding. "The economic inference at this point is that not enough has been spent on elementary schooling relative to expenditure on higher education." (*Human Resources*, p. 32) Given the changes in economic structure over the past nearly forty years, it is unclear whether and to what extent his estimates would hold good in the current economic situation.

22. Foucault, *The Birth of Biopolitics*, pp. 259–60.

23. Becker, Gary, "The Economic Way of Looking at Life," p. 38.

24. Becker, "The Economic Way of Looking at Life," p. 43.

25. Becker, Gary, "An Economic Analysis of Fertility," in *The Economic Approach to Human Behavior* (Chicago: University of Chicago Press, 1976), p. 193.

26. Becker, Gary, "A Theory of the Allocation of Time," *The Economic Journal*, Vol. 75, No. 299, September 1965, p. 498.

27. Becker, Gary. *Human Capital*, third edition (Chicago: University of Chicago Press, 1993), p. 51.

28. Becker, *Human Capital*, p. 53.

29. Bronner, Ethan, "College Students Aiming for High Marks in Income," *New York Times*, January 12, 1998, http://query.nytimes.com/gst/fullpage.html?res=9901E3DE1539F931A25752C0A96E958260&scp=2&sq=college%20students%20%22meaningful%20philosophy%20of%20life%22&st=cse (accessed December 6, 2010)

30. See, for example, his article "Altruism, Egoism, and Genetic Fitness," in *The Economic Approach to Human Behavior*.

31. Friedman, Milton. "The Social Responsibility of Business Is to Increase its Profits." *New York Times Magazine*, September 13, 1970.

32. Friedman, Milton. *Capitalism and Freedom* (Chicago: University of Chicago Press, 1982 [1962]), pp. 199–200.

33. Posner, Richard, *Sex and Reason* (Cambridge: Harvard University Press, 1992), p. 111.

34. Becker, Gary, *A Treatise on the Family* (Cambridge: Harvard University Press, 1981), p. 182.

35. Brown, Wendy, "Neoliberalism and the End of Liberal Democracy," in *Edgework: Critical Essays on Knowledge and Politics* (Princeton: Princeton University Press, 2005), p. 42. This essay also presents an enlightening summary of Foucault's treatment of *homo oeconomicus* in its relation to neoliberalism.

36. Bauman, Zygmunt, *Liquid Love: On the Frailty of Human Bonds* (Cambridge: Polity Press, 2003), pp. 42–43.

FOUR

Varieties of Friendship

Inhabiting the figures we described in the previous chapter is more than a matter of how one behaves in a particular area of one's life. One is not an entrepreneur only while at work and entirely divorced from it in one's outside practices and relations. In his novel *Great Expectations*, Charles Dickens offers us the character of Wemmick, who is a hard and difficult personage at work, but who gradually sheds his personage as he walks further away from his office when the day is done to offer a more generous and wise personality by the time he reaches home. In turn, on the way back to work, "By degrees, Wemmick got dryer and harder as we went along, and his mouth tightened into a post office again."[1]

This is an attractive model for divesting oneself of the vestiges of an unattractive area of one's life, but for most of us it is psychologically unrealistic. It is particularly unrealistic when it comes to the figures we have described. To be one of these figures is not simply to engage in activities that involve consuming or entrepreneurship. It is to identify oneself in the terms we have described in the previous chapter. Wemmick may shed his work identity as he gains literal distance on his work, but the reason for this is that he rejects that identity. He sees himself as having to don a work identity as he does his work clothes, neither of which really fit him.

We recognize this in looking around at the people we know. When I was younger I worked as a nurse's aide in an inpatient psychiatric hospital. I spend my time among psychiatrists and psychiatric nurses, both at the hospital and often socializing away from it. Although we left work when our shifts were over, work never entirely left us. We often analyzed one another's psychological motives. Moreover, we looked at human interaction in predominantly psychological terms, as opposed to political or economic or social ones. This bleeding over of one's vocational orientation into the rest of one's life is not restricted to those who work in psychology. Lawyers can be legalistic outside of their practice. Philosophers, as I have also seen, tend to approach their lives in terms of distinctions that often don't matter to non-philosophers. Athletes (as well as others in competitive professions) carry their competition off the field with them; and, as the news often reports, athletes in the more martial sports often have difficulty in separating their athletic wars from their personal and interpersonal lives. And, in keeping with what we have just said, the more one identifies with an arena in one's life—we might say, the more *figural* that arena is for one—the more profuse the bleeding from that arena into others.

However, to claim that the elements of a figure are not isolated, that they cannot be relegated to this or that corner of one's life, is not to claim that one is nothing other than that figure. As we have seen, the delinquent or the consumer is not simply a delinquent or a consumer. In order to understand the place of these figures in our lives, we have to see them as at once significant, pervasive, and not exhaustive. They are significant because they largely structure who we are and how we see ourselves. They are pervasive because, inasmuch as they are reinforced by the social, political, and economic norms of a culture, they spread themselves across our lives, seeping into the various crevices of our existence. But no culture is so totalitarian that it can enforce its norms across our entire existence or can make of us nothing more than instantiations of particular themes. To be a figure is not to be a puppet. Figures may dominate us in various ways, so that to one extent or another we become them. (Recall that, in contrast to Weber's ideal types, figures have a real existence.) To become a figure, however, is not to become nothing other than that figure. If that were the case, resistance to particular norms or cultural configurations would be impossible, not simply because resistance would be suppressed but because those norms or cultural configurations would be entirely embraced.

There are, then, two thoughts we must bear in mind as we approach the issue of friendship. The first is that our *figural* existence is not isolated to a particular arena of our lives; the second is that the pervasiveness of a figure in our lives does not entirely define us. We are never entirely other than the figures we become, but neither are we ever entirely those figures. This chapter is motivated by those two thoughts. The first leads us to understand that our relationships with others are not immune to the forces we have described in the previous chapter. The second leads us to the idea that our relationships need not be entirely circumscribed by those forces. There is, or at least can be, in our relationships the ability to resist the figures of neoliberalism.

The set of relationships we are interested in here is that of friendships. I want to make no claim that friendships are the only set of social relationships that display the pervasiveness and yet the non-exhaustiveness of the consumer and the entrepreneur. The reason for choosing friendship is not that it is a privileged area either of domination by neoliberal figures or of resistance to them. Instead, it is that friendship is a common aspect of human life, and its commonality allows us both a way to see how pervasive the figures of neoliberalism can be, and, more important, how close we often are to resisting those figures even when we don't recognize it. Most of us have friends, and at least some of those friendships have elements that are implicit struggles against neoliberalism. Resistance to neoliberalism, which is often thought to be difficult or even impossible, is closer at hand than we might think. The following chapter will detail the relationship between friendship and resistance. Here we must ask a more philosophical question. We must ask about the character of friendship and the variety of forms it takes. This will lead us to understand certain friendships as neoliberal ones and others as something deeper. It is those deeper friendships upon which the resistance to neoliberalism rests—not because they seek to resist it, but simply because they are deep friendships.

No discussion of friendship can commence without referring to Aristotle's treatment of the issue in Books VIII and IX of his *Nicomachean Ethics*. It remains a treasure trove of insights into the different paths friendship can follow. Philosophical reflections on friendship usually start with a reference to Aristotle, either to mine its insights or at least to pay homage to its legacy. Fortunately for us, Aristotle's discussion of different types of friendship is as relevant today as it was in Athens in the fifth century B.C.E., so we can take it as a model for the development of our own discussion.

For Aristotle, friendship (in the Greek the term is *philia*, which connotes a wider array of interpersonal bonds than those we would normally call friendship, but this difference is not relevant for us) is of three types. The first two types are friendships of usefulness and those of pleasure. "Now, when the motive of the affection is usefulness, the partners do not feel affection for one another *per se* but in terms of the good accruing to each from the other. The same is also true of those whose friendship is based on pleasure: we love witty people not for what they are, but for the pleasure they bring us."[2] In illustrating these kinds of friendships, Aristotle notes that the former is more common among the elderly. This is because the elderly, being frail, are often in need of the kind of benefits conferred by friendships of usefulness. On the other hand, friendships of pleasure are more common among the young, who have not yet developed the maturity to move beyond seeking pleasurable experiences.

In coming to understand these two types of friendships, the key element is what they share with each other. Friendships of usefulness and of pleasure are not concerned with the friend *per se*, with her life or her flourishing, but with what the friend offers. A friendship of usefulness does not require that either end of the friendship is attached to the other in her being, but only that the other brings benefit. The same is true of friendships of pleasure. To put this idea in the terms we discussed in the previous chapter, friendships of usefulness are both individualist and egoist. That they are egoist is clear; a friend has value only inasmuch as she is of use or generates pleasure. By the same token, they are also individualist. This is because friendships of these two types do not lie in the bond that exists between two people, but rather in what is happening at each pole of the friendship.

To recognize this, we should bear in mind Aristotle's claim that neither of these friendships is rooted in the other *as another person*. It is, instead, founded in what that person generates. Had someone else been able to generate the same use or pleasure, she would have served the friendship just as well. In friendships of usefulness or pleasure, I see things only from my own side. In this sense, I do not even see the other, the friend. I see only what she brings me. There is no tie between me and my friend. There is a bond, but it is not between two people. It is instead between one person and the good offered or generated by the other. It may well be that the befriended also feels the same way, but this will still not generate an interpersonal bond. Instead of a bond between two people each of whom enjoys the usefulness or pleasure of the other, there are two bonds standing side by side, each of which is between one of the friends and the good brought by the other.

Aristotle contrasts these two types of friendship with a third kind, true friendship. In his view, true friendship can only exist between virtuous people, "and therefore is rare, since such men are few."[3] To grasp this claim fully, we would need to have a more comprehensive understanding of Aristotle's view of virtue. While this is valuable on its own we need not linger over it here, since we will borrow only particular elements from Aristotle's account of true friendship in articulating the kinds of friendships that resist the figures of neoliberalism. In particular, we want to retain the central idea that there are certain friendships that are concerned with the other for the sake of the other. As Aristotle trenchantly puts the point, "Those who wish for their friends' good for their friends' sake are friends in the truest sense, since their attitude is determined by what their friends are and not by incidental considerations."[4] In contrast to friendships of usefulness or pleasure, true friendships require a bond between friends, in which one is concerned with the other for the other's sake.

One might see, at least in a broad sense, why Aristotle would require that what he calls true friendships would require that each of the friends be virtuous. To care for the other for the other's sake can only occur if one can step outside oneself and one's own needs, that is to move beyond individualism and egoism. This, in turn, seems to require a certain strength of character. If I approach a potential friendship motivated only by need, then it would seem that I could not care about the other for her own sake. I would be a depleted vessel, seeking in the other my own satiation. Alternatively, if I am, to one degree or another, self-sufficient, then it is easier for me to see the other in her own terms, rather than through the eyes of my own desires or compulsions. In this case, I am a full vessel that can now overflow into the other. In Aristotle's view, a virtuous person is, among other things, to a large degree self-sufficient (although not so self-sufficient as to be independent of the need for friendship). Therefore, a virtuous person is more likely to engage in a true friendship than a non-virtuous one. Further, if the friendship is to be a true one, it must develop a bond that exists in which each friend cares about the other. This, in turn, requires that each side of the friendship must have a virtuous person. For true friendships, then, there must be two virtuous people and a bond developed between them. This is why true friendships are so rare.

It is not clear to me, however, that friendships in which one cares for the other for the sake of the other require any significant degree of self-sufficiency. The idea that one must be self-sufficient in order to care for another for her own sake, while attractive, seems to me to be a mistaken idea. We all know of people who are deeply flawed, people whom we would never hold up as models of virtue or even self-sufficiency, who care for another person for her own sake. It could be a child from an impoverished environment who develops an intense bond with a care-taker or a peer, and who would sacrifice herself for the sake of that person. Or it could be a parent who, while profoundly neurotic herself, ensures that her child does not suffer the same obsessions that have marred her life. Or it could be an alcoholic who recognizes the effects of her alcoholism on a long-standing friend and arranges things such that the friend never encounters her in an inebriated state. While we might be tempted to think that one must be self-sufficient in order to reach out to others for their own sake, it is probably truer to say that what is required for such reaching out is only that one really cares about the other. This caring can happen among those who are self-sufficient, and perhaps more easily among them. But self-sufficiency is not necessary. As other writers on friendship have noted (including the philosopher Elizabeth Telfer whom we will discuss later in the chapter), friendship is such that it can be at once deep and between people who are not admirable.

The significance of the idea that one does not have to be virtuous in order to have a "true" or deep friendship is twofold. First, the kind of purity that Aristotle describes in what he thinks of as true friendship seems nearly unattainable for most of us. As the philosopher Alexander Nehamas has recently written, "for Aristotle most of us are actually friendless," at least when it comes to genuine *philia*.[5] If we are to think of some among our friendships as more than superficial, we need to break with the thought that deep friendships require some kind of personal purity. To be sure, one cannot be utterly self-involved and be capable of a deep friendship. In that sense, it is a condition for a deep friendship that one be capable of concern for the sake of another. However, there is a far distance from that condition to the purity of the virtuous.

Second, and related to this, Aristotle's requirement of virtuous people for deep friendships seems to remove people from the influence of their social conditions. As we argued in the previous chapter, people are partly a product of the societies in which they develop and exist. This does not mean that they are merely reflections of those societies; it means that they cannot extricate themselves entirely from the conditions in which they were raised and in which they find themselves. Those societies set terms, perspectives, and orientations that frame the way the issues of one's life appear to one, and even when one rejects one or another of these terms, perspectives, and conditions, one borrows from *somewhere*, at least in part, the means and/or the motivations for that rejection. At moments in his writings, Aristotle seems to recognize this. He denies, for instance, that it is likely one could become virtuous in a society in which virtue never makes an appearance. However, his reliance on virtuous people for true friendship and his concession that this implies that true friendship is rare seems to remove friendship from the often flawed conditions through which we navigate our lives.

One might want to take this point and return to our earlier discussion of friendships of usefulness and pleasure in order to undermine the stark terms in which they are presented. That is to say, just as deep friendship might come from less-than-virtuous partners, might not friendships of usefulness and pleasure also involve elements of concern for another person in herself? If we reject purity in the one case, should we not reject it in the other two? Of course, in the first case the lack of purity was in the friend herself, while in the other two it is not the character of the friends but that of the friendship that is "impure"? But doesn't the point that we are always at least partially a product of our social situation hold equally for both? If people are molded by the conditions in which they find themselves, aren't their relationships as well? And if this is so, then wouldn't it be just as surprising to find purely instrumental relationships of usefulness and pleasure as to find entirely virtuous people for deep friendships?

The answer to these questions is, I believe, a qualified yes. Most people with whom we might have friendships of usefulness or pleasure are people about whom we care to some extent. It is not as though, for instance, if a superficial friend lost her entertainment value it would not matter to us whether she lived or died. There is at least some minimal concern for the sake of those others with whom we have formed at least superficial friendships (and even for most people with whom we have not, although probably less than for the former). Aristotle recognizes this in the case of certain friendships of pleasure, writing of young lovers that, even when the "bloom of youth passes. . . many do remain friends if, through familiarity, they have come to love each other's characters, (discovering that) their characters are alike."[6] It is difficult to imagine having a pleasant or beneficial relationship with someone without developing some fellow feeling for her, not only as a human being but as a specific person whose life has some value independently of one's own.

However, this affirmation of the "impurity" of friendships of usefulness and of pleasure is a qualified one. People's concern with others for their own sake is not a binary measure. It is not that one either is or is not concerned for the other. The point admits of the more and the less. One can be very concerned for another person, even when it is only pleasure or benefit the other brings, or one can be less so. And one of the reasons for this lies in the point upon which this discussion has rested: people are partly a product of their social conditions. If social conditions press toward more concern for the other, people will likely display more of it. They will see it modeled in others, be reinforced for displaying it themselves, recognize its display more readily, and appreciate it as a good to be promoted. Alternatively, where social conditions militate against such care or concern, one is likely to find a more egoist and individualist orientation.

Which brings us back to neoliberalism.

Many readers have probably already recognized an affinity between friendships of usefulness and pleasure, on the one hand, and the figures of the entrepreneur and the consumer, on the other. This would not be a misrecognition. Among the many aspects of Aristotle's thought relevant for contemporary life is his division of friendships into types that reflect the figures of neoliberalism. For the consumer, friendships are relationships of pleasure, bringing entertainment or diversion to one's existence. For the entrepreneur, relationships are investments; they consist of interactions with others for the sake of some future goal in which those interactions are determined by the most efficient means of reaching that goal. We might say that what neoliberalism has accomplished is to give a particular economic inflection to the two types of lesser friendships that Aristotle describes, and then to encourage us to embrace them.

Zygmunt Bauman offers a trenchant description of consumerist sexual relationships. "'Purification' of sex allows sexual practice to be adapted to such [consumerist] shopping/hiring patterns. 'Pure sex' is construed with some form of reliable money-back guarantee in view — and the partners in a 'purely sexual encounter' may feel secure, aware that 'no strings attached' compensates for the vexing frailty of their engagement."[7] The purification Bauman refers to is a purging of the emotional elements of a relationship that would create a bond between the people involved. The sexual relationship is evacuated of anything other than the pleasure it involves for both sides. And, in this example, we can think of the sides as more or less separate, having no bond between them.

One might want to balk at this example of a consumerist relationship from either of two angles. First, one might argue that sex can never be "purified" in the way Bauman describes, except in pathological instances. For most people there is at least some feeling for the other attached to sex. Nobody, or almost nobody, has sex without some feeling for the other person, even if only as another human being whose desires or emotions should not be abused. In cases where this minimal sense is lacking, what exists is not a consumer relationship but a sociopathic one.

This point can be readily conceded without harm to the example. What it indicates is that there is no "purely purified" sexuality, except in those pathological cases. Recognizing this returns us to the point made a moment ago that neither consumer nor entrepreneurial relationships should be considered purely as such. What is at issue is neither an ideal type of the kind Weber describes (since there is a reality to the consumerist element in the relationship) nor an ideality in the sense that a relationship between two people can be consumerist and nothing besides. With human relationships especially, the figures of the consumer and the entrepreneur must be seen in terms of the more and the less rather than in the binary terms of existence or non-existence. What neoliberalism accomplishes is to press the more against the limits of the less.

This begins to address the second worry that might attach to the example here. Haven't there always been sexual encounters of the type Bauman describes? Sex as a "no strings attached" relationship, either consensual or one-sided, has a long history. It does not begin with neoliberalism. So what makes Bauman's example a special one? The particularity of the relationship does not lie in its existence, but rather in its *acceptance as a consumer relationship*. To see this, we can contrast the description he offers with two other approaches to casual sex. One might be called the Victorian attitude, where casual sex would be frowned upon. Although casual sex occurs during periods of official repression, its occurrence is generally denied and, when admitted, considered to be criminal or at least unseemly. In short, "pure sex" is not accepted. Alternatively, a culture or society might accept the existence of "no strings attached" sex, but not as a consumer relationship. An example of this would be the attempt to liberate sexuality from its bourgeois constraints by the hippies of the 1960s and early 1970s. Invoking the concept of "free sex" from earlier liberationist periods, many hippie communes thought that people should express their sexuality as a matter of course rather than bound to monogamous relationships that were both stultifying and oppressive to women. This movement endorsed the practice of casual sex, but did not see it in consumerist terms, as a matter of consuming pleasure in the context of an economy of egoist entertainment.

As a side note, one might claim that the latter movement actually played into the hands of the consumerist side of capitalism, allowing it to harness sexuality in the very way Bauman describes. This would see hippie sexuality on the model of, for instance, punk music or goth counterculture, both of which arose as protests against mainstream culture but were co-opted by capitalism and sold back to the public as niche items (think torn jeans with safety pins and Hot Topic). I suspect there is something to this idea, although to investigate it would take us too far afield. What is relevant for our purposes, though, is that this co-optation would involve a revision of the hippie movement. It would not be the unfettered expression of one's sexual character that neoliberal capitalism would be selling back to us, but instead the wherewithal for various practices of pleasure without commitment.

At the heart of consumerist relationships is precisely this: pleasure without commitment. Commitment, as we will see, is in itself a challenge to the figures of neoliberalism, since it involves a dynamic that cuts against the grain of both passivity, a domination of the present, and an egoist individualism on the one hand and non-productive activity, a dominance of the future, and an individualism on the other. Regarding the figure of the consumer, what one seeks from consumerist relationships are little more than forms of pleasure, entertainment, or diversion that are on offer without having to become engaged with them in a way that would create a bond either through the building of a common past or through the responsibility for a common future. Although sex can be a striking example of such relationships, we see them more commonly among people whose relationships consist primarily in mutual participation in other consumerist activities, watching sports and shopping being perhaps foremost among these.

It might be asked at this point, and again when we discuss entrepreneurial affiliations, what the role of the various kinds of virtual relationships play in promoting or resisting the figures of neoliberalism. This is an important and elusive question, one for which it is difficult at this moment to provide a definitive answer. I am postponing the discussion of virtual relationships to a brief afterward, because, I believe, the jury is out on how virtual relationships will play out in the neoliberal period. There are some things that can be said with confidence about the framework of questions that need to be asked and about the dangers of neoliberal infiltration of virtual relationships. However, I believe that both the proponents and the detractors of virtual relationships (or, more often, relationships that are partially virtual through email and social websites) have not yet grasped the complexity of what is in play here. The reason for this is an understandable rush to judgment, one that, however, I am not at this moment prepared to join.

If consumer relationships are grounded in momentary pleasure, entrepreneurial ones are grounded in future reward. Investment in relationships yields benefits that, in turn, justify those investments. The arena in which we can most clearly discern entrepreneurial relationships is that of work, rather than among what we consider to be our friendships. One develops networks and cultivates contacts with an eye to their short- or long-term benefits for one's work projects or one's career. It might seem strange to assimilate these relationships to Aristotle's conception of friendships of usefulness, but this strangeness may dissipate a bit if we recognize two things. First, as we noted above, Aristotle's conception of *philia* casts a wider net than its English translation into *friendship*. This, however, is just a semantic point. The other and deeper issue is that the entrepreneurial approach to work relationships does not end at the borders of our jobs. We are not like Dickens' Wemmick, leaving our vocational countenance at the office. Even less so in a neoliberal society, where we are encouraged to think of our lives in terms of investment and return.

Robert Lane captures this point when he writes, "If we do not think *about* market-related things, what we do think about often (but certainly not always) reflects what we have *learned from* the market. To a large extent the assumptions that we learn are, in fact, *causal theories* about ourselves and the institutions that affect our lives."[8] Oddly, however, in another book Lane exhibits the very market approach to which he calls attention in this passage. In *The Loss of Happiness in Market Democracies*, he writes, "A further property of the two goods friendship and money is said to influence the nature of choices between them: the comparative time schedules of their yielding up their utilities. . . . Although we cringe at applying this calculating language to friendship, we nevertheless do assess our friends, although with less attention to 'value for money' and less concern for whose ledger shows a credit and whose a debit."[9] Although, as we will see in the following chapter, deep friendships can be threatened if all of the giving is on one side or another, or if there is a great imbalance of some sort in the relationship, this is a very different matter from thinking of friendships in terms of utilities and ledgers.

We also see the entrepreneurial approach to relationships in play if we recall the analyses of the entrepreneurial figure offered, with approval, by Gary Becker. To see one's spouse or one's children in terms of investments is to think about them in entrepreneurial terms. This does not exclude seeking their benefit for their sake. Altruism is not precluded by the entrepreneurial approach to relationships. But even when altruistic or concerned with the other, the entrepreneurial figure does so by means of considering the investment of time and other resources that is to be made, along with the return for others that different possible investments might yield.

Moreover, entrepreneurial concern with others is not in keeping with either the Aristotelian spirit of true friendship or the kinds of deep friendship we discuss further on in this chapter and the next. For Aristotle, to be concerned with the other in a true friendship is not simply to calculate what activities that one performs will have particular bearing on another's well-being. It is to be involved with the life and fate of the other.

This is not so much a matter of calculation (although it does not preclude calculation at particular moments) as of a non-calculative engagement with another, feeling their feelings as one's own and acting in accordance with the rhythm of the bond that arises between one and another. This is why Aristotle believes that friends must "live together," not in the sense of occupying the same dwelling but rather in the sense of spending their days together. "Now, since a man's perception that he exists is desirable, his perception of a friend's existence is desirable, too. But only by living together can the perception of a friend's existence be activated, so that it stands to reason that friends aim at living together." [10]

Aristotle does not focus on the emotional character of the bond between two friends, although emotional entwinement is central to the depth of a friendship. And this entwinement resists translation into entrepreneurial terms. To act in accordance with the emotional flow of a friendship rarely involves stepping back and asking what one should invest in order to achieve the proper good of a situation. It is more often a matter of allowing oneself to be carried along the currents of the relationship, to sense without calculation what needs to be said or done. To be with a close friend is often like being in one's own body, as in something one moves naturally, entrusting oneself to it rather than forcing or reflecting on its direction. This flow of the emotional lives of friends is not, of course, given at the outset. There may be a particular spark when future friends meet one another, a spark that seems to imply an immediate understanding. However, in order for the full depth of a friendship to develop, there has to be the thickness of time between friends that can only come, as Aristotle recognizes, by "living together." This suggests the importance of the past, of a sedimentation of time, over the course of the emergence of a deep friendship, a point to which we return below.

At this point, we are beginning to palpate aspects of friendships that are neither consumerist nor entrepreneurial. We are turning from the critical account of what neoliberalism makes of us and our relationships toward another vision of how we might be with one another. It is time, then, to take up the task of understanding friendship in different terms from those our context often offers to us. I have used the term *deep* friendships, for lack of a better one, and will continue to invoke that term (or sometimes the term *close*). I hope the term does not carry too much baggage with it. There is certainly a sense in which I want to claim that the kind of friendships we are about to describe are deeper than consumerist or entrepreneurial ones. The connection between people who are involved in what I am calling deep friendships is tighter, their bond more profound, than friendships founded either in pleasure or usefulness. However, one might want to say, for instance, that a person can be deeply invested in another as a useful friend, meaning it in the sense that one has put much of her resources into that friend and is reliant on the friend to achieve the good she seeks. I do not want to argue that the depth of deep friendships is somehow deeper than the depth of this entrepreneu-rial reliance. The depth of a deep friendship is something that is lived between people more than measured as a quantity.

In order to approach these sorts of friendships, it would be worth beginning with a particular concept of trust. This is not the trust to be found in the deep friendships themselves, but rather in a more pedestrian relationship, that of telling something to one another. This may seem to be an unpromising place to begin a discussion of trust. However, by starting here we can accomplish two tasks. First, we can see how trust is rooted in our fundamental relationships with one another. Second, and related, by finding trust among the most basic of our relationships, we can recognize that the elements of resistance to the figures of neoliberal-ism are not far to seek, but are instead lodged in the most common of our interactions with one another.

In two articles recently published independently of each other, the philosophers Edward Hinchman and Richard Moran discuss the particu-lar type of speech known as *telling*. When I tell something to someone, I do more than just announce it, assert it, or say it. To tell someone, for instance, that it's raining outside or that Foucault's lectures on sexuality describe four figures is not merely to put a claim in public space for assessment. Moreover, my telling someone something doesn't just give her evidence that it's true. When I tell someone that it's raining outside, there is more going on than her thinking to herself, "Well, he told me it's raining so it's more likely to be raining than not." The title of Hinchman's article, "Telling as Inviting to Trust," suggests that above and beyond evidential considerations, there is a personal relation that seeks to be established through the act of telling. As he argues, "She intends that his entitlement to believe that p derive not merely from the fact that she spoke but from the fact that she addressed him in such a way as to engender a trust relation—that is, from the conjunctive fact that she told him that p *and that he trusts her.*"[11]

What is this trust that is added to the fact of telling, or better is added to the fact of a saying in order to produce a telling? "Trust, we can say generally, is a species of willed dependence, where the dependence is under appropriate guidance of a counterfactual sensitivity to evidence of untrustworthiness in the trusted."[12] In other words, to trust someone, in the absence of reasons not to trust her (i.e., "a counterfactual sensitivity to evidence of untrustworthiness") is to put oneself in the position of de-pending upon the other for the truth of what is told. When you tell me it is raining outside, you ask me to not only to believe that it is raining outside, but to believe it *because you told me so.* To tell someone something is to invite them into a particular relation with the teller, where what is told stands not simply as a claim to be believed but as the offer of a bond between the one who tells and the one who is told.

We might think of the difference between telling, and, say, asserting, this way. In asserting, I put a claim out in public space as an individual occupying that space. I am a member of a particular speech community, and as that member I add or suggest something to the stock of knowledge of that community. Other members of the community might choose to believe what I have said for any number of reasons. They might have independent evidence of my assertion, or they might recognize that what I assert often turns out to be true, or they might be too lazy or too busy to investigate the assertion for themselves. None of these constitute a relation of telling in the sense Hinchman and Moran discuss. In all of these cases, the members of the speech community are in an important way isolated from one another and from me. What is said does not serve to bind them to me. It serves only to add to their stock of knowledge (or, if false, not add to it). Even where the evaluator decides to believe the assertion because of my reliability, no relation is established between her and me. My reliability might as well be that of a weather vane. Weather vanes are reliable indicators of wind direction, but nobody would be tempted to develop a relationship with a weather vane on that basis.

What telling adds to assertion, as Hinchman and Moran point out, is the binding relation of trust. As Moran says, "The speaker is asking that a certain authority of his be acknowledged—the authority to invest his utterance with a particular epistemic import—and this investment occurs by his explicit assumption of responsibility for his utterance's being a reason for belief. . . the recognition of intention *enhances* rather than detracts from the epistemic status of the phenomenon (utterance)..."[13] In telling someone that it's raining outside, I take responsibility for that other person's belief. On the other side of things, that person, if she does not reject my telling, trusts my intention and thereby makes the fact that I have told her it's raining with the intention of her believing it to give her *more* of a reason to believe that, in fact, it's raining outside. The epistemic authority of her belief, her entitlement to believe it, stems not merely from the words or from any evidence of me as a reliable assertor, but from the bond that is established between my telling and her trust.

People tell us things all the time, and we often believe them. We believe them not only because we're lazy, or because otherwise there would too much to investigate on our own. It's certainly true that there is much we have to take on faith. If we stopped to investigate every claim that came before us, we'd never get anything done. But often our believing is not simply a matter of convenience. We believe people because they have told us something, and we trust that they would not tell us this if they were not in a position to know it. We believe, not just what they have said, but *them* in their telling of it. Without this relation of trust, the social bonds between and among us would be much thinner than they are.

Relations established by telling, then, while not universal, are certainly common. Trust—at least the minimal trust required by a telling relation—is ubiquitous. Its ubiquity also cuts against the figures of neoliberalism, precisely at their joint commitment to individualism. Recall that for both the consumer and the entrepreneur, one's relation to others is an individualist one. The other is not someone to whom I bind myself, but rather someone from whom I either consume pleasure or invest time and other resources. Neoliberalism sees a world of isolated individuals occasionally coming into contact, like pool balls, but retaining intact surfaces. There is no room in the neoliberal figures for the pedestrian occurrence of telling, because there is no room in neoliberalism for relations of trust between people. Just as neoliberal economics leaves everyone on her own to fend for herself, so the figures of neoliberalism—that is to say, who we are inasmuch as we are products of neoliberalism—are isolated one from another, each in her own world. The borders of those worlds may touch, but they do not interpenetrate.

One might want to say here that if this is true, then there must be, even in the neoliberal world, more than the figures of neoliberalism can accommodate. Indeed it is true, and it is the point we're driving at. There are basic relations we have with one another, relations that cut against the grain of neoliberalism. Even if, to one extent or another, we are the products of neoliberalism, its figures, we are never only that. And we are never only that in some of the most primitive of our relations to one another. This implies two things. First, who we are with one another provides a wellspring for resistance to the figures of neoliberalism. Otherwise put, neoliberalism violates the sources of who we are with one another, and because of this our relationships with one another, in their very being, resist neoliberalism. Second, and on the other hand, the stronger neoliberalism is, the more it constitutes a threat to those sources. Inasmuch as we take on the characteristics of the figures of neoliberalism, the ties that bind us to one another become frayed. The trust that we confer on one another, our "willed dependence," seems to be less a source of social glue and instead evidence of naïvete or nostalgia. (We will return to this idea in the next chapter.)

The trust requested in telling and acknowledged when one agrees to be told is, of course, not yet friendship. People can tell us things who are not our friends. When the train conductor tells me that we'll reach my station in ten minutes, I trust him on this, but my trust does not make us friends. Friendships involve both more trust than this and more than just trust. However, trust is a central element of deep or close friendships. It is part of the bond that keeps friends together, and is bound to the history of particular friendships, a theme we will discuss at some length. We might say that part of the soil of friendships lies in telling and being told, but that the soil is not the plant itself. Instead, friendship nourishes itself on the nutrient of trust.

How might we define friendship above and beyond trust? There are, no doubt, many ways to do so. For our purposes, the goal is not the precision of the definition itself, but rather the ability of the definition to allow us an entry into an understanding of deep friendships, particularly as they contrast with friendships of pleasure and utility in their contemporary guise: friendships of consumer pleasure and entrepreneurial benefit. I draw a fruitful definition of friendship from Elizabeth Telfer's classic 1970 article entit'ed, simply, "Friendship." She writes that, "there are three necessary conditions for friendship: shared activities, the passions of friendship, and acknowledgement of the fulfillment of the first two conditions."[14] Before delving into the particular matter of deep friendships, let us pause to consider the elements of the definition.

The first condition, that of shared activities, recalls of course Aristotle's view that friends share their lives together. This seems a fairly obvious criterion of friendship. It is hard to imagine using the term friendship among those who are not engaged in any kind of shared activities. We will return in the appendix at the end of the book to the question of whether that sharing requires contiguity in time and place. If it does, then there cannot be online friendships; but if not, then there can. Nevertheless, it is difficult to imagine friendships in which no activities are shared. This includes not only deep or close friendships, but also friendships of pleasure and use. The former kinds of friends can hang out at the mall together or play video games, while the latter might interact as professional conferences or business meetings, sharing a drink or planning a strategy for mutual gain.

In a recent article, sociologists Scott Feld and William Carter have emphasized this aspect of friendships. They note that friendships tend to arise around what they call "foci of activity." "A focus of activity is defined as 'any social, psychological, legal, or physical entity around which joint activities are organized.'"[15] Friendships, in other words, do not arise in a vacuum. Instead, the emergence of friendships occurs because of a particular social context in which organized activity is occurring, whether social, vocational, or otherwise. This, they note, has implications for the character of the friendship. Just as friendships do not arise within a vacuum, they are not maintained in one. The norms of the friendship often reflect the norms of the joint activity in which the friendship arose in the first place. "[W]e suggest that the nature of the embeddedness of most personal relationships is primarily determined by the foci of activity in which the relationships originated and secondarily determined by later shared involvements in foci of activity."[16]

The significance of this suggestion is twofold. First, as the authors emphasize, the initial context of a friendship is importantly determinative of its future course. This does not mean that what happens later can be predicted from a knowledge of that context. Rather, the norms that particular friendships follow, the interests that are focused on, and the style of the friendship borrow from and never lose their moorings in the initial foci of activity in which the friendship is rooted. As Feld and Carter comment, "the norms applying to friendships arising out of an adolescent church group are likely to be substantially different from those arising out of a video arcade."[17] Moreover, a friendship arising from a church group will carry those norms within it, even though it may develop other norms, "secondarily," if the friendship persists through other foci of activity.

The endurance of the initial foci of activity and its norms is not difficult to discern in friendships. It is hard to imagine a friendship that would so entirely shed its early identity that it becomes something wholly other than what it once was. This is not to say that one cannot imagine this in some logical sense, but rather that one cannot easily imagine it with one's own friendships. For instance, I have a friend with whom I have been close for over forty years. We have spent most of those years living in different cities, and so have developed different networks of friends. Nevertheless, we relate to each other in much the same ways we did when we met. Our conversational duels regarding which of us can be more ironic, our underlying common search for meaning, our often unstated but palpable concern for each other's vulnerabilities: these are all thematic and normative aspects that have persevered since high school. And, in a less central way, we periodically return to elements of our shared past. We were both runners, both had the same mentor, and both had a peculiar attachment to New York as a defining city for our lives. (The return to these themes, if it becomes a dominant aspect of the relationship, can often tilt the friendship toward the nostalgic, which is either a sign of a dying friendship or at least of a friendship where the past has overwhelmed the present and future. Tom Waits' song "A Sight for Sore Eyes" captures this nostalgia poignantly.)

The other significant aspect of this suggestion is one that we have already hinted at and will treat in more detail below. In contrast to the consumerist focus on the present and the entrepreneurial focus on the future, the character of a deep or close friendship relies in an important way on the past. Feld and Carter suggest that one of reasons for this importance is the role played by the context of the initial activities and norm in which the friendship is immersed. As William Faulkner reminds us, "The past is never dead. It's not even past." This is as true of interpersonal relationships as it is of the burden of larger historical legacies.

The second condition for friendship, the passions of friendship, involves what Telfer calls an affection for the friend. More than that, however, she adds that that affection is not necessarily rooted in the particular character of the friend. In other words, it is not the qualities of a friend that are the object of passion in the affection of friendship, but the friend himself or herself. She adds, not disapprovingly, that, "Affection is in this sense *irrational*, and because of this may survive radical changes in the character of its object. Thus we often continue to be fond of someone when we no longer like or respect him, and such a situation is not considered in any way odd."[18] As Telfer argues, this irrationality of friendship goes against the Aristotelian idea that true friendships can be had only among good people, that is, people of good character. The passions of friendship allow the impoverished child, the neurotic mother, and the alcoholic we mentioned earlier to overcome their weaknesses of character and develop deep friendships. On the other hand, and closer to Telfer's point, it might also allow people to become friends or to sustain a friendship with them.

What might it mean to say that affection is irrational, particularly in this latter case? It does not mean that affection is crazy or entirely out of someone's control. Rather, the idea is that it does not necessarily follow reflective considerations. I am friends with people with whom I might, if I reflected about it—or even if I do reflect about it—think that I should not be friends with. Telfer offers the example of friends who change, but whom one still likes. This can be someone who, for instance, brings one alive because of her vitality and willingness to bend the rules, but who later expresses the same quality through self-destructive behavior. We might still feel affection for her, might still consider her a friend, even though we feel we shouldn't.

At first glance this could seem to be a puzzling element of friendship. It shouldn't. Over the course of time, people change in a variety of ways. If it were impossible for friendships to follow those changes, friendship itself would be only a passing phenomenon. In order for friendship to survive, it must be able to sustain itself over the course of personal changes. Some of these changes might lead to a loss of respect for the friend. But, as Telfer points out, a loss of respect does not necessarily entail a loss of affection. (Part of the reason for this may lie in the persistence of the norms derived from the initial foci of activity insisted upon by Feld and Carter.)

However, we should not take this to mean that all friendships necessarily survive all changes. In order for the affection of friendship to sustain itself, there must be someplace where that affection can hang its hat. If the friend of two paragraphs ago who was vital and bent the rules became self-destructive and at the same time began to be sapped of her vitality, our affection for her might diminish as well. (It might not, but it might.) Perhaps it would be replaced by pity, or, depending on the circumstances, disdain. Again, the irrationality of affection in friendship is not utter mindlessness; it is more restrained than that. It is instead the resistance of that affection to be entirely harnessed to reflective considerations.

The irrationality of affection appears to cut against one of the friendships we have discussed: entrepreneurial friendship. And indeed it does. The passions of friendship, inasmuch as they do not respond to reflective considerations of utility (whether the utility of self-interest or of altruism), are diminished in Aristotelian friendships of utility. When I seek to maximize a particular good through friendship, I do not allow my affection for the friend to stand in the way of the rational calculation of the use of that person for the good after which I strive. Does this mean either that friendships of usefulness are not really friendships, or alternatively that Telfer has given us too constricted a view of friendship? I think that neither is the case. Friendships of usefulness do involve some degree of affection, even if it is more constrained than that the passion of a true friendship. If there were no affection, we would likely be hesitant to call the relationship a friendship. As we saw above, friendships of pleasure and utility ought not to be considered purely as matters of one or the other. There is a qualified impurity to these friendships. There arise in friendships human feelings that bind people together. Neoliberalism, inasmuch as it molds us into its figures, pushes against those human feelings, and may succeed in stunting them. If it were to succeed entirely in doing so, we would probably say, not that friendships had fallen under the sway of neoliberal individualism, but that there was no longer any such thing as friendship. But that, fortunately, is not our situation.

What Telfer has accomplished with her reference to the passions of friendship, then, is to isolate a necessary characteristic of friendship that appears in a more full-blooded way in deep friendships and more anemically in our friendships inasmuch as we are either entrepreneurial or consumerist. Otherwise put, she has recognized that all friendships involve affection, and in doing so has also—although this is not her concern—laid the groundwork for distinguishing deep or close friendships from neoliberal ones.

The final condition of friendship is an acknowledgement of these first two conditions. That is, friendship does not simply involve a sharing and a passion, but also some recognition that these are in place. Another term she uses for this acknowledgement is commitment. A friendship is not based on the happenstance of sharing and passion, one that seems no more than a stroke of good luck. Rather, it also involves what we might call a tending to, in the sense that one tends to one's garden. There is an awareness of the special relationship a friendship involves, one that calls one toward the other as a matter not only of passion or affection but also of cognitive commitment. This tending to a relationship involves a recognition of the role of the past, of the personal history of friends, that we will return to below.

Before developing further the conception of friendship, and in particular of deep friendships, we might pause a moment over the historical character of friendships. In the second chapter, we saw that who we are is not immune to the historical conditions in which we live. Neither are our relationships. It might seem, then, that friendships as Telfer describes them would also be historical phenomena. Friendships that involve the kinds of sharing and passion she describes might be a product of particular historical conditions rather than a universal human style of relationship. In fact, this has been argued by the sociologist Ray Pahl in his book *On Friendship*. His claim, against those who would say that capitalist society has diminished friendship, is that it is rather capitalism that permits it. "Those who argue for the commodification of social relationships, a retreat to a privatized home world and the growth of a new rational calculus, seeing social cohesion in terms of analogies with economic theories of exchange, have perhaps been prone to assertion rather than to a careful consideration of the evidence." Pahl relies here on the historical research of Alan Silver, who claims that it is the rise of commercial societies that allows friendships to arise outside of the impersonal arena of the market. According to Pahl, "it was precisely the spread of market exchange in the eighteenth century that led to the development of new benevolent bonds."[19]

In the introduction to their collection, *Placing Friendship in Context*, Rebecca Adams and Graham Allen point out that Silver's claim is a controversial one, although they insist—as the title to their book would indicate—that friendship is not immune to historical influence. "While Lopata, for example, suggested that the development of commercial society led to a decline in the social significance and heterogeneity of friendship, Silver argued that commercial society actually encouraged friendship by ridding ties of the 'contamination' of instrumentality."[20] This argument might have bearing on our discussion in two ways. First, and more narrowly, it raises the question of the relation of an exchange society to the entrepreneurial figure of neoliberalism. Second, and more relevant for the purposes of this chapter, it asks after the historical character of friendship itself.

The first question can be answered briefly. It might well be that the emergence of early capitalist society freed relationships from some of their moorings in feudalism and allowed for the cultivation of non-instrumental forms of friendship. We in the neoliberal period, however, do not find ourselves in a time of the emergence of capitalist society. If the rise of commercial society as Pahl and Silver see it is the groundwork for friendships in a non-entrepreneurial mode, then it is one of the ironies of neoliberalism that, in pushing capitalism to its limits, it has undermined the freeing of friendship that it earlier encouraged. This would be one of those historical ironies to which the philosopher Hegel calls our attention, one in which the internal development of a phenomenon leads to reversing the very character of the phenomenon itself.

The second question is whether friendship as described by Telfer is itself historically situated. Were there friendships that did not involve shared activity, passion, and a recognition of these? Moreover, might it be that the character of deep friendships, which we have only begun to suggest, varies from one historical period to another. Although there is likely to be some variance, I am skeptical that the general outlines of Telfer's conception of friendship or of the character of deep friendships will be utterly different from what we have seen or will see. Part of the reason for this is historical, but partly it is a philosophical matter as well. Historically, we have already seen that the different kinds of friendship described by Aristotle are not only recognizable; they have contemporary resonance. And, as Pahl concedes in discussing the emergence of non-exchange friendships during the early capitalist period, "Aristotelian styles of friendship re-emerged with the coming of commercial-industrial society in the eighteenth century."[21] The persistence of these kinds of friendships suggests that there is something more to friendship above and beyond its social and historical embeddedness. This point can be recognized even while conceding the importance of Feld and Carter's insistence on the importance of the foci of activity and their norms for particular friendships. The character of friendship as described by Telfer does not need to deny that importance, but only to place it within a framework that can make friendship recognizable across historical periods.

This leads to the philosophical (or perhaps semantic) reason why friendships or even deep friendships cannot be utterly different from what has been and is going to be said about them here. A relationship that did not involve any shared activity or passion would likely not, in our view, be called a friendship. Even if the people involved in that relationship called it a friendship, I think our response would be to say that they are mistaken about the term. There are many ways in which people relate to one another. We reserve the term friendship for a particular set of those relationships. Even though the borders of that set may be fuzzy, there are many kinds of relationships that clearly lie outside those borders. If we were to look in the past or in some geographically remote area and discover a social grouping in which none of the relationships met something like Telfer's definition (or another suitable definition) of friendship, we would likely say that within that group the bond of friendship does not exist. This seems to me to be the right way to characterize the situation.[22]

NOTES

1. Dickens, Charles, *Great Expectations* (New York: New American Library, 1963 [1867]), p. 228.
2. Aristotle, *Nicomachean Ethics* tr. Martin Oswald. (Indianapolis: Bobbs-Merrill, 1962), p. 218 (1156a10–15).
3. Aristotle, *Nicomachean Ethics*, p. 220 (1156b25).
4. Aristotle, *Nicomachean Ethics*, pp. 219–20 (1156b10).
5. Nehamas, Alexander, "The Good of Friendship," *Proceedings of the Aristotelian Society*, Vol. 90, Part 3, October 2010, p. 274.

6. Aristotle, *Nicomachean Ethics*, p. 221 (1157a10). This is not a concession he makes to relationships of usefulness. The passage cited continues, "But when it is the useful and not the pleasant that is exchanged in a love affair, the partners are less truly friends and their friendship is less durable. Those whose friendship is based on the useful dissolve it as soon as it ceases to be to their advantage."

7. Bauman, *Liquid Love*, p. 50.

8. Lane, *The Market Experience*, p. 26.

9. Lane, *The Loss of Happiness in Market Democracies*, p. 97.

10. Aristotle, *Nicomachean Ethics*, p. 271 (1171b30)

11. Hinchman, Edward, "Telling as Inviting to Trust," *Philosophy and Phenomenological Research*, Vol. 70, No. 3, May 2005, p. 577.

12. Hinchman, "Telling as Inviting to Trust," p. 578.

13. Moran, Richard, "Getting Told and Being Believed," *Philosopher's Imprint*, Vol. 5, No. 5, August 2005, p. 18.

14. Telfer, Elizabeth, "Friendship," in Pakaluk, Michael (ed.), *Other Selves: Philosophers on Friendship* (Indianapolis: Hackett, 1991), p. 257.

15. Feld, Scott, and Carter, William C., "Foci of activity as changing contexts for friendship," in Adams, Rebecca G., and Allan, Graham, *Placing Friendship in Context* (Cambridge: Cambridge University Press, 1998), p. 136. The citation within this citation refers to an earlier invocation of this definition by Feld.

16. Feld and Carter, "Foci of activity as changing contexts for friendship," p. 142.

17. Feld and Carter, "Foci of activity as changing contexts for friendship," p. 141.

18. Telfer, "Friendship," p. 252.

19. Pahl, Ray, *On Friendship* (London: Polity Press, 2000), p. 54.

20. Adams, Rebecca G., and Allan, Graham, "Contextualizing Friendship," in *Placing Friendship in Context* (Cambridge: Cambridge University Press, 1998), p. 11.

21. Pahl, Ray, *On Friendship*, pp. 53–54.

22. The philosopher Tyler Burge offers a rigorous defense of this way of using terms in "Individualism and the Mental," *Midwest Studies in Philosophy*, Vol. 4, No. 1, 1979, pp. 73–122.

FIVE

Deep Friendships

What Telfer's definition has accomplished is to isolate, among our personal relationships, a set that involves more than passing acquaintanceship or professional engagement. These are our friendships. In our discussion of her isolation of these relationships, we have already suggested three elements that are central to the character of deep friendships: regard for the other, passion, and the role of the relationship's past. We will focus on each of these, and in addition add a fourth: the meaningfulness of a deep or close friendship.

First, a deep friendship is, we might say, other-regarding. That is to say, friendships, at least the ones most of us admire, to one degree or another seek the good of the other for the sake of the other, and not simply for one's own sake. This, we saw, is perhaps the most important characteristic of friendship that Aristotle uses to distinguish true friendships from friendships of pleasure or of utility. It is also found in other accounts of friendship, for instance when Cicero writes, "we do not exercise kindness and generosity in order that we may put in a claim for gratitude; we do not make our feelings of affection into a business proposition. No, there is something in our nature that impels us to open hand and heart."[1] In some friendships there may be an orientation toward the friend that, we might say, pulls us off the center of ourselves, allowing us to expend ourselves on behalf of the friend. This element of deep friendship already largely distinguishes it from friendships of pleasure and from most entrepreneurial friendships. Entrepreneurial friendships can be altruistic, as we have seen, but neoliberalism presses them in the direction of self-interest. In both types of friendship, regard for the other is minimal. It would not figure in a description of these friendships that sought to isolate their salient characteristics.

However, it is certainly possible for relationships to be other-regarding without being friendships. There are people on whose behalf we act, either because we feel we owe them a debt, say of gratitude, or because we are being altruistic, or because we feel it is our duty to help them. Unless one is committed to a view of people as psychologically egoistic, acting only on behalf of their own interests, one can see that there are many ways of being other-regarding, only some of which arise in the context of friendship. And, since in philosophy at least (and I believe, although I'm no expert on this, in psychology as well) a thoroughgoing psychological egoism is no longer taken seriously as an account of human motivation, then we can see other-regardingness at work in a variety of relationships. One of the elements that must be added to regard for the other, or better entwined with it, is what Telfer calls passion or affection.

Almost all friendships involve some degree of affection, even if it is minimal. We have seen that friends, even when they are primarily concerned with their own pleasure or benefit, often display some positive feeling toward the other. But, as with regard for the other, this degree of affection is less of a defining characteristic than a supplement to the friendship. In deep or close friendships, the passion one has toward the other is one of its central characteristics. In approaching this affection, Telfer uses the common term "liking." And she says of liking that it is directed not toward particular characteristics of the person, but toward the person herself. An account of liking that would focus on particular personal characteristics "tends to suggest that before we can like someone we have to tot up items in his nature and strike a balance between the attractive and unattractive aspects of it. But in reality our reaction, like a reaction to a picture, is to a whole personality seen as a unified thing."[2] Although Telfer believes that liking characterizes all friendship, the significance of liking for deep friendships is far more central than for the neoliberal friendships of pleasure or utility.

This liking for the whole person has at least three implications that are particularly relevant for a deep friendship. First, it reinforces Telfer's claim that friendship can be had not only among Aristotle's virtuous. If a deep friendship required one to be able to "tot up the items" in the nature of the other, and if that balance struck was unfavorable—as it would be with someone who was not virtuous—that would preclude friendships of any depth with that person. Friendships, though, and especially deep friendships, are more holistic than that. It is not difficult to see why. If one were friends only on the basis of particular characteristics of the friend, it would not be the person herself that would be the object of the liking, but something about them that could be instantiated just as easily in others. This would lead in two directions, neither of which we would call paths of deep friendship. First, the idea of characteristics as the object of liking tilts toward consumerist or entrepreneurial relationships. Some particular aspect of the other brings one pleasure or is useful to one. That is a matter, not of a bond to the other, but of an individualistic use of the other for one's own ends. This tilting can be distinguished from a necessary condition; it is possible to like an isolated characteristic of the other for its own sake and without regard to one's ends. But one can see the easy slippage from focusing on characteristics to a certain self-serving-ness.

The other direction that a focus on characteristics would lead to is that of the replaceability of friends. If it were not the whole person herself, but only the attractive aspects of her personality, that were the object of the liking, then it would be entirely possible to replace that friendship with another one just like it for someone who possessed or displayed the same characteristics. But friendships don't have that kind of replaceability. We will see why not further on, when we discuss the role of the past in the place of deep relationships.

To say that deep friendships involve a liking for the whole person, and not just a particular set of characteristics, does not preclude us from articulating things we happen to like about that person. One finds a friend to be charming or interesting or generous, and likes that about her. There may even be aspects of a friend one likes without being able to give a precise description of or name to that aspect. A friend may have a way of looking at you when you talk, or a particular tone to her voice, that draws you to her. But in the end it is the person, not the sum of the characteristics, that one likes in a friendship. In fact, the tone of voice that one may be drawn to in a friend, for instance, could seem repulsive in someone one didn't respect.

This leads to the second implication of the liking of the whole person: it has a certain non-cognitive character. By that I mean that in liking a whole person, one cannot give an exhaustive account of what it is one likes in liking a friend. Telfer tells us that, "Liking is a difficult phenomenon to analyse... It seems rather to be a quasi-aesthetic attitude, roughly specifiable as 'finding a person to one's taste,' and depends partly on such things as his physical appearance, mannerisms, voice and speech and style of life; partly on his traits of character, moral and other."[3] Telfer insists, as we just saw, that liking a friend does not mean one takes an inventory of these things. Instead, they somehow meld into a person to whom we are drawn. It is the whole of these (and perhaps other) elements, the way they are combined in this particular person, that we like in a friend, rather than any grid or table of the elements and their combination.[4]

The non-cognitive character of friendship would seem to be more characteristic of deeper friendships than of shallower ones, and especially the neoliberal friendships of pleasure and investment. With the latter in particular, there is often a particular element or group of elements that one invests in with a particular gain in mind. One is drawn to the intelligence or charm of another, hoping to learn from it; or one admires her ability to take charge of a situation, and seeks to use that ability for one's own ends. One does not generally invest in, as Telfer says, "a difficult phenomenon to analyse." Regarding friendships of pleasure, the case is more complicated. It surely seems possible to say that the liking for a whole person rests on her giving one pleasure, without being able to say what exactly it is that generates the pleasure. More often, though, it is particular characteristics that yield pleasure, whether wit or wealth or physical prowess or a specifiable sum or combination of these. One usually takes pleasure, not in the person herself, but in particular aspects of that person. Of course, a deep friendship, as we have seen, can also take pleasure in specifiable aspects of the person. But above and beyond that there is a liking for the whole person that often distinguishes a deep or close friendship from one rooted primarily in pleasure.

The third implication of a liking for the whole person is that one wants to be with that person, to share time with her. If what one liked were only a characteristic of that person, then one might want only to be around that characteristic, and might equally enjoy being around it when it in someone else. And there are certainly characteristics like these. I enjoy a quick wit, and enjoy being around it even among people I don't particularly like. But with a friendship, and particularly a deep friendship, what one wants to be around is the person herself. Recall Aristotle's insistence that friends must live together. "Now, since a man's perception that he exists is desirable, his perception of a friend's existence is desirable, too. But only by living together can the perception of a friend's existence be activated, so that it stands to reason that friends aim at living together." When we first cited this passage, we saw it in connection with the non-calculative engagement with the other that true friendships involve. Friends live together because that is what a non-calculative emotional engagement is. Here we can see another dimension to this non-calculative engagement. It rests on a liking for the whole person, one that leads person to want to be around the friend: not around this or that aspect of the friend, but around the friend herself. One wants to spend time with her, to share her company.

This "desire for the other's company,"[5] as Telfer puts it, or for "living together," according to Aristotle, involves a different type of non-calculative aspects of friendship from the one mentioned in the earlier citation of the passage. The earlier non-calculative aspect has to do with the fact that in wanting to share the company of a friend, one does not ask oneself how much time one should spend in order to yield a specific benefit. The liking of the whole person indicates another non-calculative aspect, one that we have called non-cognitive. Especially with deep friends, not only does one not calculate how much time to spend with the friend on the basis of its yield, one also cannot exhaustively specify what it is about the friend that draws one to her company. Close friendships are often doubly vague. They involve a desire to be around the other that is uncertain in both the character of the time spent and the reason for spending it. An account cannot be given; one is left with the sense that there is a hole near the center of one's words.

Although vague or elusive, these aspects do not render deep friendships mysterious in some mystical sense. We know what we are talking about here, since we often experience it with our closest friends. There are people with whom we like to spend time and whom we miss when we don't spend time with them. We feel that their company is not only enjoyable, but meaningful to us. Being with them is part of what our lives involve, part of what it is for us to be living *this* life as opposed to another. We don't calculate how much time or for what reason we want to be with these friends. There may be particular activities that we enjoy together, perhaps those related to the initial grounding of the friendships. In the end, however, it is not only the activities themselves that matter, but the friends with whom we engage in them. And if asked we will likely have a hard time giving a satisfying account of why it is we want to spend time with the other. It is not that we are reduced to silence. We could say *something* about why we like sharing our time with the friend. But any account will seem to fall short of the place in our lives that spending time with the other occupies. (This is one aspect of Montaigne's dictum at the end of his essay on friendship that, "If you press me to say why I loved him, I can say no more than because it was he, because it was I." We will see another aspect below, when we return to the irreplaceability of friends.) This is not because friendships rest upon or are rooted in some ineffable or unfathomable mystery. It is, rather, because deep friendships are not the object of a calculation regarding the time spent together, and because friendship is for the whole person, and indeed that whole particular person herself, rather than some characteristic or combination of characteristics.

So far we have discussed two aspects of deep friendships: they are other-regarding, and they involve passion or liking. These aspects are not separate from each other. It is not that I have a respect for the other's person, and then in addition happen to like her. Instead, the two are entwined. I regard the other's interests as important because I am drawn to her as a friend, and my being drawn in this way is intensified the more I see her as person whose perspective, interests, and desires are worthy of my respect. This is one of the dynamics of a developing friendship, one that can emerge from either aspect (or both at the same time). Let's say, for instance, that I find myself liking someone, wanting to be around her for reasons that I can partially but not entirely account for to myself. Perhaps I use words that may serve more as gestures or placeholders than as real explanations. I say to myself that she's interesting or intelligent or charming. In liking this person, I come to regard her viewpoints as important ones, worth taking into account. From there, it is only a short step for her desires and interests to begin to matter to me, not because they might further any projects of mine (even the project of developing the friendship), but simply because they are hers.

From the other end, one can imagine a friendship that begins in respect. I have a close friend who is a lawyer, and whom I first saw when he testified on behalf of me and a number of other folks who were on trial for an act of civil disobedience. (I hasten to add here that the trial was in front of a magistrate and for a misdemeanor.) I was struck by his articulateness and commitment and developed a regard for him both as a lawyer and an activist. Because I was new to this community of organizing, and because he had an elevated reputation in that community, my respect for him was held at a certain personal distance. Over time, however, we began to get to know each other, and a mutual liking developed. This mutual likened has blossomed into a personal intimacy that remains between us. In return, this intimacy reinforces the regard I have for who he is. It makes me take seriously both his views (especially his political views) and the ways I might intervene in order to enhance the trajectory of his life.

The third aspect of friendship we indicated above was the role played by the past. This role is actually a complex one, tied not only to the historical character of any deep friendship but to issues of trust and the irreplaceability of friends. In order to approach it, it might be best to start with the writer Graham Little's discussion of what he calls communicating friendships in his book *Friendship: Being Ourselves with Others*. Like Aristotle, Little divides friendship into three types. These types overlap with Aristotle's but do not coincide with them. Little calls these types *social*, *familiar*, and *communicating*. He defines social friendships as "an adjunct to organised social relations. Though freer than many relationships, social friendship takes its cue from the goals and standards of the wider society. It appears as group morale on the job and in recreations like sport; easygoing friendliness among people of the same type, class, nation, gender; fraternisation and comradeship; a rest period from duty and criticism, a drink with the boys."[6] Social friendships are the most superficial of the three, yet they hold a place of significance in our interpersonal relationships; they are often the oil that greases the way for us to navigate the world without friction among us.

Of social friendship, Little writes that it "is often grudging, shallow, conformist, flat-footed and even hypocritical. Social friends are afraid of friendship and aren't really interested."[7] This is hardly a ringing endorsement of social friendship. However, the contrast Little makes here is with communicating friendships, to which we will return momentarily. Social friendships, although often cursory, are, like Aristotle's friendships of pleasure, a necessary component of human life in society. The fact is that we cannot be close friends with everyone, and yet this does not entail that we cannot be friends with them at all. There are people around us whose company we enjoy, whom we have some affection and care for, and this is as far as matters need to go. Social friendships flow with the normative social codes in which they arise; recreational friends, for instance, observe the norms of the athletics they're engaged in, not only in terms of the rules of the games themselves but also of the unwritten rules that govern these friendships. And they need not be more than that (and cannot be more than that for *everyone* with whom one is friends). As Little recognizes, social friendship "sometimes expresses the sort of realism that knows that no amount of friendship will bring us all to heaven together."[8] If the choice is between being alone among many of the others with whom we share the world and developing some social friendships that cannot be more than social, there is something to be said for the latter.

Social friendships resemble Aristotle's friendships of pleasure in their superficiality and in their making us feel more comfortable with one another. In addition, friendships of pleasure take place largely within an unquestioned set of social norms. After all, to challenge those norms would likely involve one in an unpleasurable experience. Moreover, as Little points out in his discussion of communicating friends, a deeper friendship has the resources to challenge norms in a way that shallower ones do not. However, social friendships and friendships of pleasure are not identical. Social friends need not be entirely about pleasure. A social friendship can occur where there is no pleasure involved. Little offers an example. "Rita, a young nurse, pretends her very sick patients are friends while she keeps it in mind that they will pass through her hands to die: 'I like nursing so much because you walk into the ward and the people, the patients, are so willing to give to you. There's no gradual build-up of a friendship. Suddenly you treat them as friends, you talk to them, and then you leave.'"[9] What characterizes social friendships, then, is less the pleasure they bring (although most of them will bring the kind of pleasure Aristotle envisions) than the social normative constraints within which they occur and through which they help one navigate.

Little defines his second type of friendship, familiar friendship, as "the attempt to reproduce for adults what an ideal family would be like for children. It offers help, comfort and continuity. It is opposed to the requirements of society, or is at least a haven from them. Christian friendship, emphasising charity, neighborliness and brotherly love, is an example of the familiar type."[10] Key to familiar friendship is the response to vulnerability, or, from the side of the person responding, the need to feel oneself as offering help. Little remarks, "In a roomful of familiar friends, if I wasn't sick, wasn't broke and not more than usually down in the dumps, I might go out looking for social friends. . . familiar friends are also afraid that their caring isn't needed. Independent, busy, healthy people, who don't know they're unhappy, who take their friends for granted, and who enjoy friendship's lighter sides, are a worry to familiar friends."Little, *Friendship*, p. 105.

Familiar friendship may seem less like friendship and more like nursing or caretaking. We can, however, see our way to recognizing the friendship nature of familiar friends. There are people of whom we say, "I can be myself in front of her." Often, we don't mean by this that with others we are entirely pretense, or that somehow we are more really what we are in front of these friends. We mean that we can be weaker in their presence, less guarded and more exposed in our emotions. We trust that the friend will, at the very least, not betray our vulnerability, and more likely will support us in it. In fact, with such friends it becomes part of the character of the friendship that there is this exposure, often mutually. When this exposure is not occurring or seems not to be needed, as Little points out, it can feel as though there is something wrong or missing in the friendship.

Many readers will already have noticed the similarity between familiar friendship and Aristotle's friendships of usefulness. In both types of friendship there is a reliance on the other that is central to the identity of the particular friendship. Familiar friendships are, I believe, a subset of friendships of usefulness. They are those friendships where vulnerability is a prominent or even the central theme of the relationship. While friendships of usefulness can be based on vulnerability, the category has a wider scope. Entrepreneurial friends, for instance, are friends of usefulness in Aristotle's sense without being familiar friends in Little's. In fact, for entrepreneurial friends, displays of vulnerability or personal exposure would most likely be deterrents to the development of the friendship. What entrepreneurs seek are go-getters, not support systems.

There is something particularly modern about familiar friends, something that perhaps would not be as readily recognizable in Aristotle's time. Familiar friendships are partially grounded in the public/private distinction that has evolved over the course of the past several hundred years. This is the distinction between what happens in the arena of socially common space and what happens outside of it, for instance in the domestic sphere. There is, of course, much to be said about this distinction, which has always existed in some form but has become more prominent with the rise of modern democracies and their emphasis on more widespread political deliberation and decision-making. Many feminists, for instance, have discussed how the distinction reinforces traditional gender roles, allocating public space to men while relegating women to the private sphere. In this way decisions about the shape of the society, which are made in the public political sphere, are put beyond the scope of women's participation. (Of course, this relegation has a long history. The distinction between public and private is simply one of its more recent incarnations.) In another way, the role of economics in relation to the public/private distinction is an important one. Is economics, as capitalism would have it, largely a private matter? Or, as socialists claim, should decisions about the structure and ownership of an economy be answerable to public deliberation? For our purposes, the significance of the distinction, although inseparable from these other aspects of it, lies within the way it divides one's public from one's private self. We display aspects of ourselves in our general social dealings—including those that Little calls social friendships—that are different from those we display more privately. In particular, most of us are likely to put on a show of strength in the public sphere (however defined) that we do not feel the need to display among certain of our friends. Those friends are, to one extent or another, familiar friends. They are the people in front of whom we let down our defenses, those with whom we shed our public personas as we do our work clothes. And if they are more thoroughly our familiar friends, they are those with whom we share the insecurities, worries, and weaknesses that we have kept under wraps during our sojourn through public space.

Are social and familiar friendships really friendships, or are they some other form of relationship? I don't see any bar to calling them friendships. They certainly meet Telfer's definition. They involve shared activities, even when those activities are—as they often are in familiar friendships—largely conversational. They also involve passion or liking. And, since these friendships are voluntary, they include a recognition of the shared activities and the emotional connection. One might want to ask whether familiar friendships, when they arise in the context of familial relationships, should be thought of as something other than friendships. Little seems to preclude familial familiar friendships when he refers to them as attempts to "reproduce" ideal family structures. This raises the larger question of whether family relationships of any kind can be characterized as friendships. For our purposes, nothing of significance hangs on this. There is no bar to allowing friendship to include family relationships when they meet the description we have offered here. What we are interested in are not the borders of the use of the term *friendship* but rather the kinds of relationships we have and can have with one another, particularly in the economic age that is our current ether.

Little's third type of friendship, communicating friends, is his equivalent to Aristotle's true friendships. "Communicating friendship, the pure type, is built on exchanges that stimulate hope and invite change. It is about knowing and being known, about communicating singular identities. This is the friendship the Greeks gave us, an ideal type which offers a win-win result where everybody grows and expands in each others' interests."[11] We might think of the ideal type Little mentions as a Weberian one, but we need not. Rather, we can think of communicating friends, like other categories we have invoked throughout, as a matter of the more and the less. Communicating friends interact with each other in ways that involve both deeper levels of sharing and mutual knowledge and self-knowledge. Communicating friends both understand and change one another, and these two aspects of friendship interact.

To understand what Little is on about here, we might begin by asking why he uses the term *communicating* friends? "Pure friendship is called communicating friendship because, as Aristotle puts it, 'in the first place friendship is a communication or partnership.' The chief activity of friends is 'conversing and exchanging ideas' and what they communicate above all is their consciousness of themselves and each other; the exchange of self-insights is the reason for their friendship...The heart of friendship is not companionship or sympathy. . . but mutual self-awareness."[12] Communicating friends offer each other (or one another—there is no need for friendships to be exclusively dyadic) self-understandings that work both to develop each friend's knowledge of herself and, partly as a consequence, to lead to the growth of each.

We might deepen our understanding of this dynamic of self-knowledge and growth by looking at a recent discussion of Aristotle's conception of true friendship. The philosopher Talbot Brewer claims that true friendship, what he calls "character" friendship, centrally involves the development of *universally self-affirming evaluative outlooks.* "Let us use the phrase 'evaluative outlook' to refer to a person's characteristic sense of the evaluative features of actual or possible human doings."[13] An evaluative outlook is a normative outlook upon oneself and the world; it is the perspective within which one sees goodness and badness in what is happening around one and one's own place and role in these happenings. An evaluative outlook is the normative lens through which the world makes sense not only in an explanatory way but also and more important in terms of oughts and ought-nots.

An evaluative outlook is self-affirming under the condition that "when it brings its own verdicts or other manifestations into view, it is invariably able to approve of them."[14] An evaluative outlook is self-affirming when we are okay with what it is telling us. This is not a difficult criterion to meet. When we reflect on our normative perspective on the world, we often approve of it. The real challenge lies in the universality of this self-affirmation. "An outlook is universally self-affirmable if it affirms all possible embodiments of the same outlook, whether in its possessor or in others."[15] Can I affirm my evaluative outlook in all of its aspects not only when I reflect on it but moreover when I see everyone else around me acting on the basis of the same outlook? That is the question of universal self-affirmation of evaluative outlooks.

In order to grasp the idea, we can use an example of an evaluative outlook that would *not* be universally self-affirming. There are people who think that foreigners should be treated less well than one's national compatriots. This is, of course, not an entire evaluative outlook, but only an element of one. It is also clearly self-affirming; many people do affirm it in themselves. In fact, they affirm it with their fellow compatriots. But is it universally self-affirming? No. One would not endorse this attitude if it appeared in those foreigners, and especially if it was directed toward oneself. Many people would chafe under the treatment by foreigners that they commend with regard to them. And again, this is something we see regularly. While a number of people who call themselves patriots are happy to exclude the native languages of foreigners from public discourse, they are offended when those foreigners are engaged in conversation in their native language within earshot. Why? They feel excluded or threatened in the very way they recommend treating those very conversationalists.

For most of us, probably almost all of us, there are elements or aspects of our evaluative outlooks that would not pass the test of universal self-affirmability. Or to put it in other terms, there are ways we could develop better evaluative outlooks. This, in turn, would make us into better people, because we would be looking on the world—and acting within it—in ways that took not only our own desires into account but also the interests and desires of others. The question might arise of how we go about the process of maturation of our evaluative outlook. We could reflect on it, and this would surely help. However, it is easy when reflecting to miss some aspect of how we're thinking or to let ourselves off the hook or to deceive ourselves about our own evaluative prowess. It would help to have another perspective on the matter, a perspective that comes from someone else with whom we could share our outlook and who could, in both word and deed, help us recognize how we're looking at things and what the implications of that looking are. In short, we could use communicating (or what Brewer calls *character*) friends.

Brewer writes, "such friendships will be marked by conversation about matters of importance to them both, and these conversations will presumably help participants to become more articulate about the best and most laudable patterns of human activity and interactivity, and to correct for idiosyncratic blind spots in their appreciation of these activities."[16] When I talk with a close friend about matters of importance to me, or see her in action embodying something I admire, or find myself saying sharing some grievance with her that seems to become petty to me even as I verbalize it, or listen while she explains patiently why I really don't believe what I said I believed, or hear myself explain the same to her and in my speech realize that I am guilty of the same disbelief on other areas: when these things happen, I grow. I become a better person. And I do so in ways that would not have occurred without my relation to this friend.

Communicating friends are those through and with whom we develop ourselves, each other, and one another. This development cannot occur with social friends or with familiar friendship. Social friends do not have the depth of relationship that would foster self-development. Conversations are not deep or prolonged enough, and one doesn't expose one's vulnerabilities to those with whom one has a more passing acquaintance. Familiar friends, in their turn, are likely to sacrifice development and challenge for solace and succor. One shares with a familiar friend more of oneself than with a social friend. But the point of the sharing is not challenge or growth but acceptance. In neither of these types of friendship is there likely to be the kind of sustained conversation and mutual self-reflection that would lead to the growth of evaluative outlooks.

There is another aspect to communicating friendship, one that is crucial for the discussion of the following chapter. Little tells us, "Communicating friendship becomes utopian and radical because, being about identity and invention, it must conflict with existing norms."[17] Communicating friendship offers challenges not only to the character of the friends— by deepening and altering their evaluative outlooks. In the same gesture, it can also challenge the social norms within which communicating friendship takes place. To see why this is, we can contrast the dynamic of communicating friends with that of social friends.

Social friends conform to the current social normative structure. They must. The point of social friendships is the smooth navigation of that normative structure. My beer drinking buddies, if that is all they are, are people with whom I quaff a few brews, tell a few jokes, discuss sports, and maybe drive home if one of them has gone too deep into her cups. If I were to ask them to reflect with me on my evaluative outlook or share the lingering regrets of my life, they would likely become uncomfortable. If I kept this up, I would have to find new beer drinking buddies. There are ways such buddies act. Everyone knows this. To act contrary to this is to challenge the social norms of this particular practice.

However, not all drinking buddies stay just that. There can be the occasional buddy with whom I might sense a potential for something deeper. Maybe when the others have trotted off to the bathroom, we have a short conversation about something more significant than sports or alcohol. Maybe we recognize an emptiness in each other's lives that each has hidden largely from our friends, or even from ourselves. This may turn into a communicating friendship. But what happens to the norms of beer drinking when this friendship arises? Perhaps nothing. But we may find that the norms of those nights of drinking are not enough, that they are too superficial. One of us might, even without prior discussion with the other, try to introduce more personal topics into the conversation. She or I might raise the topic of unfulfilled lives, and the fear and loneliness they bring. The reason this could happen is that, through our communicating friendship, each of us has, while still enjoying the company of other drinking buddies, found the superficiality of the conversation oppressive or constraining. We like these buddies, but have begun to recognize that there is too much significant human interaction precluded by the norms under which we have been acting. We like our drinking buddies, but we would like our friendships with them to have more substance than they do.

This is a modest example. It seeks only to show how in an everyday way communicating friendship can challenge existing norms. Little writes, "Pure friendship is an alternative to society, a platform for criticising it, for social and moral invention and individually chosen lines of self-improvement."[18] This allows for much more profound social challenges than the norms of bar conversation. A friend who reveals to a close friend that she is gay challenges that friend's evaluative outlook and perhaps invites her to "moral invention." Friends that decide that social authority is demeaning and commit to constructing a cooperative dedicated to alternative and more egalitarian lifestyles are engaged in the kind of "social" invention Little describes. This happens because when friends communicate in an open way—not just for the purposes of acceptance characteristic of familiar friends—it is unclear where that communication will lead. To offer one's evaluative outlook for consideration is to place oneself in uncertainty, an uncertainty whose resolution may land one in a very different place from which one started.

It may seem as though communicating friendships are predominantly friendships of self-reflection, personal development, and challenge. A reading of Aristotle, and of Brewer's interpretation of Aristotle, would reinforce this impression. Little, too, when he claims that, "The heart of friendship is not companionship or sympathy. . . but mutual self-awareness." His use of the terms *companionship* and *sympathy* are directed toward the other two types of friendship. However, the distinctions between these two phenomena and deep friendships are too sharply drawn. Deep friendships, what Little calls communicating friendships, involve companionship and sympathy as well, not simply as adjuncts to a friendship but as central contributants to it.

The reason for this has partially—but only partially—been given. Close friends, as Aristotle insisted, must live together. They must spend time in companionship with each other or one another. Without this time spent together, there cannot develop the bond that allows for the mutual self-reflection, growth, and personal invention. Not only that, time spent together is valuable in itself. When I am with a close friend, our time together assumes a significance for me that is difficult to articulate, but that nevertheless I would be impoverished without. We might better understand the role of sympathy and companionship in deep friendships if we use different terms to discuss them. For sympathy, we can return to the concept of trust. For companionship, we should ask about the role of the past in the constitution and sustenance of a deep or close friendship.

We have already met the phenomenon of trust in discussing Moran's and Hinchman's treatments of telling. We saw there that telling involves a trust of the other that is from one side a dependence on the teller and from the other an assumption of responsibility. To trust another who is telling one something is not simply to believe that it is likely that the other is correct. It is to trust *her*, in her person, to lay oneself epistemically before her. Similarly, to ask for trust in telling goes beyond putting some information in front of the other; it is to request a personal relationship by taking up the responsibility for what is told. Telling, because it involves trust, establishes bonds between people that, as we saw, challenge the individualism characteristic of the figures of neoliberalism.

The trust involved in deep friendships has the same structure as the trust required by telling, but it is more intense and sustained. It should not be surprising that it has a similar structure. After all, one of the themes of communicating friends is that they communicate: they tell each other (or one another) things, about themselves, one another, the world, values, etc. The conversational development of evaluative outlooks, for instance, cannot occur without a lot of telling. And that telling, precisely because it is telling, requires trust of the friend with whom one is in conversation. But consider this. Sometimes people who dislike you or who are indifferent to you will say things to you that are at once true and uncomfortable. You may even recognize the truth in what they have said, but you discount it. A close friend might say the same thing to you and it would matter more. You're more likely to consider it and consider yourself in light of it. The difference between your friend and those who dislike you lies in trust. It does not lie in the information being revealed, in what is communicated to you. It cannot, since it is the same information in either case. It is rather that you trust the friend, you place yourself in a position of dependence on the friend that you would not consider doing with someone less interested in who you are and might become. In Hinchman's more technical rendering, "in declining S's invitation A treats S's telling as a telling he merely hears, or overhears, not as a telling addressed to him. In other words, he treats S's telling as a mere assertion."[19]

The more intimate or vulnerable the aspect of oneself that is at stake, the more trust is required in order to place that aspect up for discussion or reflection. This is why deep friendships require a greater degree or intensity of trust. If one of the distinctions between social friends and close or communicating friends lies in the reflective consideration of one's evaluative outlook, one's normative take on the world and oneself, then the stakes are higher with close friends. This requires a higher level of trust. It might be argued that familiar friends also require a higher level of trust. As with communicating friends, one is revealing intimate aspects of oneself to the friend, which opens the possibility for abuse of one's vulnerabilities. The difference, however, lies in the prospect of telling that is involved. Familiar friends do not tell one anything about oneself that might be difficult or uncomfortable to hear or that might lead to self-evaluation. And one doesn't ask that of familiar friends. One only asks acceptance for who one is, for a blind embrace.

However, the distinction between this blind embrace and the trust involved in deep friendships is not as clearly demarcated as Little seems to suggest. The embrace required for a deep friendship may not be blind, but it is an embrace, and a sympathetic one. One cannot trust a friend for certain kinds of telling unless one feels assured that one is accepted by the friend, that one's well-being matters to her. As Little himself says of communicating friendship, "it welcomes the different ways people are alive to life and tolerates much in a friend for the sake of his best intentions."[20] Now to be fair to Little, he does say that in communicating friendships sympathy and companionship "are likely to be involved" even if the are not the "heart" of such a friendship. However, this hierarchical relationship between sympathy and trust on the one hand and communication on the other seems foreign to deep friendships. Trust and sympathy are not only instrumental to the self-development of friends; they are a crucial aspect of the friendship itself, contributing in their own right to the meaningfulness of the friendship. It may be true that a friendship that rests solely on sympathy and without the possibility of growth and development cannot rise to the level of a close or communicating friendship. However, it is unlikely that a relationship that fails to sustain itself through the sympathetic and trusting relationship of its participants is likely to be considered much of a friendship at all.

The reason for this lies in the element of companionship that deep friendships require. And this element, in turn, reflects a temporal significance to the past in deep friendship that goes missing in relationships of neoliberal figures.

As we have seen, the figure of the consumer is oriented toward the present. That is where the pleasure is. The figure of the entrepreneur, by contrast, is oriented toward the future, which is where the profit is. For neither figure does the past play a significant role. There is no pleasure or entertainment in the past, and nothing to be gained from a past that is no longer. Deep friendships, by contrast, require a past. The past does not have to be temporally extended: deep friendships can develop through a short but intense past. For there to be a deep friendship, however, the past must play a founding role. The role it plays is not a nostalgic one; in fact, nostalgia often replaces communication in friendships that once might have been deep. Rather, its role is that of foundation for the friendship itself.

This is one of the subtlest lessons of Aristotle's claim that true friends must live together. The kind of trust required for the development of a deep friendship does not just happen. Although having a friend, unlike a family member, is voluntary, it is not voluntary in the way that choosing what one is to have for lunch is voluntary. There may be, and often is, a spark that flashes between people who are later to become close friends. This spark is not the friendship itself, but only a promissory note. Moreover, choosing to follow the suggestion of that spark is not yet the friendship either. It is in the actual following of the spark, in the time spent together after the spark, that the deep friendship develops. Companionship is essential for the emergence of deep friendship. Otherwise, the development of a degree of trust that is significantly greater than the trust involved solely in telling cannot occur.

One of the reasons for this is obvious. I cannot trust someone to any significant degree if either I do not know who she is or feel that she does not know who I am. Otherwise, I would just as well trust a stranger. But to know who someone is, and to allow oneself to be known, takes time. Again, that time can be telescoped into a shorter period with intensely developed friendships. But the friendship that occurs emerges from that time and is always rooted in it. We have already seen one of the elements of the rootedness: the foci of activity in which friendships arise. And, at least according to Feld and Carter, friendships never entirely shed the framework of those foci of activity in which they are initially founded. The themes of this common focus offer a basis for trust that is developed over the course of a relationship.

If this were all, then the trust characteristic of friendships would be static. It would lie solely in the initial phase of the relationship and be carried through it untouched by the time that followed. We know deep friendships are not like this. However indebted a friendship is to its beginnings, it must be animated by the time lived together between those beginnings and its present state. There is a vitality to time spent together that molds and re-molds its initial phases, adding dimensions to the friendship that were not present in its earliest incarnation. To be involved in a deep friendship is to be part of a temporal process, a process that does not simply unfold what was there in germ at the outset, but that instead creates what will be there through conversation and shared activity. It is this process, and the bond that is created through it, that intensifies the trust between friends from something like the more superficial trust involved in telling to a trust in which evaluative outlooks, vulnerabilities, intimate emotions, and tentative hopes can be shared and reflected upon.

Imagine a close friendship of long standing. Three people meet in high school through participation in a common activity, say athletics or a club. In the initial phases of their friendship, they develop an interpersonal style of conversational humor punctuated by occasional sharing of their dreams and their fears. They come from successful families, and are expected to sustain that success. They are not sure they want to, though. Their parents' success sometimes looks empty to them, and for one of them the success seems inseparable from the distance in her parents' marriage. They graduate high school and go to different colleges, but maintain contact. The friend with the distant parents goes through a period of intense alienation and drinks too much. The other two friends visit with her occasionally and talk with each other about how to help this friend during this difficult period. They sometimes feel at sea with this, knowing that the friend would prefer that they not contact her parents, but not knowing what else to do besides spending time and offering advice and encouragement. Eventually, the friend finds her way, they all graduate, and go on to separate careers.

Later, another of the friends is herself involved in a loveless marriage. Her husband is, while not abusive, at best discouraging of her career and even her person. This friend would like to leave the marriage, but is not sure of herself outside its context. She is not even sure she deserves better. Her friends challenge her, first to stand up to her husband, and if that doesn't work to divorce him. She is not capable of the former, but eventually succeeds in the latter. This leads to a period of loneliness, during which her friends offer encouragement. In the end she never re-marries, finding life on her own with the occasional lover to be preferable to a stable relationship where she is afraid she will submit her own pro-jects to that of her husband.

The third friend is offered a position at a prestigious university teach-ing English. She is ambivalent about taking the offer, knowing how much work it will involve and insecure about her ability to meet the demands it requires. Her two friends diverge in their view of whether she should take this position. One of them thinks she is just underestimating herself; she needs to jump in with both feet. The other one believes she will not enjoy being overwhelmed with work, and that her outside life is too significant to be sacrificed for the demands of the position. They all talk. She takes the position, but later quits it, deciding that she had succumbed to the seduction of peer recognition rather than understanding that she found more meaning in balancing her work with her outside life. Later she wonders whether she was right in quitting. Throughout, the friends continue to disagree, but support her in her tacking back and forth.

Over the course of this trilateral friendship, one can further imagine the persistence of the initial foci of activity. The friends might still engage in the activities through which they met. They occasionally run together or play chess or do whatever it was that brought them together in the first place. They carry on a conversational style that is mostly humorous. But their interaction, and the trust arising from it, has become magnified over the years. Their shared experiences and the thickness of the time over which this sharing has occurred has allowed them to trust one another even where they disagree. Without this time, their trust would not have risen to the level to which it has. They would not be able to reflect upon their various evaluative outlooks and shape them over the years.

That is not all. What I said in the previous paragraph is consistent with the idea that the primary activity of deep friendship is "mutual self-awareness" and personal development. Sympathy and companionship would be in the service of these. But to reduce their friendship to this, I think, would be a misrepresentation of the character of this friendship. Over the course of their time together, these friends have certainly en-gaged in such self-awareness, reflection, and growth. And these have been predicated on a trust that has become deeper with the time they have spent together. However, these aspects of the friendship would hardly be called definitive of it. They enjoyed their time together, they empathize with the trajectories of one another's lives, and this enjoyment and empathy is not just subsidiary to their personal growth.

We might put the point this way. While we would hesitate to call their friendships deep ones if they were unable to contribute to the personal growth of one another, particularly at the crucial moments of despair, divorce, and career choice, we would equally hesitate to call them deep if those contributions were all there were. Their time together, spent in ways that might on the surface be called social or familiar, are integral to the depth of their relationship. While communication in the way Little describes it or developing evaluative outlooks as Brewer articulates it may be a necessary characteristic of a deep friendship, it does not trump sympathy or companionship. They are both necessary for it. Moreover, they carry their own integrity in the course of close friendships.

Both sympathy and communication are rooted in the history of companionship that roots deep friendships. This history is, in each case, singular. Friendships share histories that are unique to those friendships. Although others may intersect with that history, the immersion of friends in their particular history cannot be replicated with or by anyone else. My history with a close friend, along with the trust, sympathy, and communication that we have developed over the course of it, is an essential and irreplaceable facet of our relationship. And alongside the irreplaceability of our history is the irreplaceabililty of the friend itself.

The philosopher Christopher Grau has written on this bond between history and irreplaceability in the context of love relationships, although the point holds equally for friendships. My friend cannot be replaced by another friend, even a friend who might be an identical substitute. We have already seen a related point in Telfer's discussion of liking friends as a whole. It is not, she argued, the particular qualities of friends that we like; rather it is the whole they embody that is the object of our affection. The history we share together helps explain this. My history with a friend, if it yields a deep friendship, is a history with that particular person in all of her virtues, failings, and quirks. The friendship we develop in undergoing that history together is one that binds the two of us together, both as we are and as we develop. It does not concern parts of us, but concerns each of us as a whole. Moreover, it concerns each of us in our uniqueness. Grau argues that, "in addition to obvious forward-looking aspects, many love relationships contain a genuinely backward-looking element. This is because love often involves, not just an attraction to a cluster of qualities that might be valuable in the future, but a commitment to a concrete individual who has a particular origin and a particular past—in other words, a commitment to an individual with a particular identity."[21]

Grau argues that this point undermines those who want to say that in love it is only the qualities that we love or who would argue that in a sci-fi world where one could be replaced with a identical duplicate then one would love the duplicate equally. The point to be insisted on here is that the love for another person in their uniqueness and their history, that is, their irreplaceability, emerges from the common and unique history that arises between friends. Because of our history, I come to care for someone just as she is, in the history that has made her this individual and not another. As Brewer puts the point, among what he calls character friends, "The irreplaceability of one's friends owes in part to the self-conscious *history* one shares with them, and this is not the sort of thing one could conceivably discover oneself to share with a stranger."[22] This, it seems to me, is the deep truth behind Montaigne's above-quoted remark about his friendship that "If you press me to say why I loved him, I can say no more than because it was he, because it was I."

This particular irreplaceabililty of friendships and their history contrasts sharply with the consumerist and entrepreneurial friendships of neoliberalism. Consumerist friendships are easily replaced; if one friend no longer gives pleasure or is entertaining or fun to be with, then one drops her for another. There is no deep bond tying one to consumerist friends. They are bound predominantly by enjoyment. And where enjoyment is the motive for the friendship, a lack of enjoyment can as well be the motive for its termination. As Bauman remarks of both material goods and relationships in a consumerist society, "Consumerism is not about *accumulating* goods (who gathers goods must put up as well with heavy suitcases and cluttered houses) but about *using* them and *disposing* of them after use to make room for other goods and their uses."[23]

One might argue here that although the friends are replaceable there is nevertheless, even in consumerism, an irreplaceability to the friendships themselves. It may be a superficial one, rooted only in the particular pleasures these friends share. But, one might say, consumerist friendships each partake of their particular pleasures, and no two consumerist friendships are entirely alike.

This may be true, but it would miss the point of irreplaceability we are discussing here. We have invoked the concept in two places: the irreplaceability of friends that Grau has argued for, and the unique and irreplaceable history of deep friendships. The former has to do with the uniqueness of the friend, the latter with the friend*ship*. The objection would not press against the former at all, since it concerns friendships and not the friends themselves. If it were to have bearing, it would be on the second point. However, even there it goes astray. The irreplaceability of deep friendships is rooted in a particular history of sharing and collaboration. That irreplaceability takes up significant—even central—roles in the lives of those friends and, as we will see momentarily, confers particular meanings upon them. Those roles cannot be played by others, whether strangers or more superficial friends. This irreplaceability, then, is not the uniqueness of two snowflakes or shades of blue that are not exactly alike. Such claims can be made of many things, including consumerist friendships. It is instead a matter of recognizing, beyond any superficial uniqueness, that the roles a deep friendship plays in one's life cannot be filled in another way or by another person. The loss of a consumer pleasure can be compensated for by the reception of another one. The loss of a close friend is a wound that never entirely heals. As Brewer remarks, "The loss of an intimate friends, then, is the loss of a jointly created world of significance and possible activities—a world that owes its contours to the friends' own past activities rather than to mere serendipity."[24]

Entrepreneurial friendships, for a similar reason, are also not concerned with irreplaceability. For the entrepreneur, it is the profit to be gained by a particular relationship that constitutes its justification. If that profit is no longer expected, then it is time to abandon the friendship and look for other opportunities. This does not happen with a deep friendship. It is not that deep friendships never come to an end. But when they do, it is a generally a more tortured or at least ambivalent affair. Because of the rootedness of the friendship in one's past and its contribution to one's life, the ending of a deep friendship is not simply a matter of seeking new opportunities. The loss of a close friendship is, as Brewer says about the loss of a close friend, the "the loss of a jointly created world." Although the remnants of that world in both cases may stay with one— they are sedimented in one's life the way habits become sedimented over time—without the friendship or the friend they do not animate one's life in the same way. They exist more like a wound or perhaps a scar than as a vital part of one's existence. All of this is in contrast to an entrepreneurial friendship, whose continuance is predicated on continued gain.

Another way to put this point would be to say that among deep friends there is a loyalty that goes missing among entrepreneurial friends. Loyalty in friendship is not simply a matter of duty. It does not arise simply from moral obligation. The loyalty to a close friend is at once more spontaneous and more passionate. It concerns the protection of or care for another where a threat to that friend is a threat to a shared life. This does not entail that loyalty to a close friend is egoistic. It is beyond the distinction between egoism and altruism. It stems from a desire to protect the other that is not entirely separable from a recognition that what is threatened is neither entirely hers nor mine but ours. There is no equivalent to this in entrepreneurial friendship (nor, for that matter, in consumerist friendship), because there is no bond of the kind that exists in a deep friendship. Further, there is no bond of this kind because there is no shared history to create one. The past plays no role in constituting the character of an entrepreneurial friendship. It is the future, with its expectation of gain or loss, that determines the nature and extent of such a friendship. When I network with those who can advance my career, I always have in mind what they will do for me. If they are no longer of use, they tend to fade from my awareness.

We should note, to counter the risk of misunderstanding, that these aspects of a deep friendship are compatible with tinges of ambivalence or envy toward the friend. It is difficult to imagine a deep friendship constituted solely by the characteristics we have described here. This is not only because of the individualist context in which we live, although undoubtedly that would serve to heighten any ambivalence. It is also, and in a more pedestrian way, because we are creatures often riven, to one degree or another, with ambivalence. There is no reason these would not find their way into close friendships, and there is no problem with their being there. They can exist in such friendships, as long as they are not aspects of these friendships that structure them. They are part of our all-too-human inheritance; we recognize them, and move on.[25]

We have canvassed a number of aspects of the character of a deep friendship, as well as their connections: its other-regardingness, its passion, its communicative role, its relation to the past. Before turning in the next chapter to the issue of how friendship constitutes a resistance to neoliberalism, there is one more aspect that would be worth discussion: the meaningfulness of a deep friendship. This may seem obvious, and in a sense it is. But, given the neoliberal framework in which we exist, it is worth distinguishing meaningfulness from happiness, with which it might be confused.

Happiness is a multivalent term. It is sometimes used to refer to a generally positive state of being, something like a sense of fulfillment or peace. Sometimes its reference is toward something narrower, like pleasure. In neoliberalism, particularly in the figure of the consumer, it is this narrower use that predominates. To be happy is to have pleasant or exciting experiences. This is why the consumer often needs to migrate from pleasure to pleasure. Since each pleasure fills only a slim temporal period, to be happy requires that one seek another pleasure after the glow of the previous one has faded. In speaking of meaning, there is something like the former kind of happiness involved, but there is more to it than that as well.

Deep friendships are best thought of as contributing not just (and not primarily) to the happiness of our lives but to the meaning they display, both to us and likely to others as well. To get at this idea, we can return once again to Brewer's phrase "a jointly created world." Friendships do not only intersect with one's life; they help create it. The shape a life takes is in part a product of its deep friendships. To be involved in a set of deep friendships is not simply to know certain people well. It is to participate in certain activities as opposed to others, to take on (or at least engage with) certain views of the world, to see oneself in a particular light out of which one acts, to reflect upon oneself in certain ways, to privilege one or another set of emotional relations to others, even to be in particular geographic locations as opposed to others (certain houses or bars or arenas or neighborhoods). This is not only a matter of making one happy or content; it is also a matter of the kind of life one leads.

But there is more to it than that. If this were all, then we might say that deep friendships help structure a life, but that that role could be played by other social relationships as well. One can imagine a life with only social friendships. Would these not help structure a life in at least some of the ways just listed? Although they would not reach deep into one's sense of oneself and the world, they would certain provide a venue for activities, emotions, geographic locations, in short they would give a structure to one's life. Deep or close friendships, in lending a meaningfulness to life, are more than just its structuring elements. They contribute to a sense of one's life as being worthwhile, and in two ways. First, they contribute to the vitality of a life, to its feeling to the one living it as though it is worth continuing. (This is the aspect that might get confused with happiness.) Second, they offer a justification to one's life. Not the only justification, in most cases, but certainly an important one. To be in the midst of deep friendships is to have a reason for one's life, a reason that is rooted in something other than the enjoyment one takes in oneself and one's continuing to exist.

The philosopher Susan Wolf has recently addressed the issue of meaningfulness in the aptly titled *Meaning in Life and Why it Matters*. In seeking to grasp meaningfulness in life, she offers what she calls the "fitting fulfillment" view. This view has two sides, each corresponding to one of the terms. On the one hand, a meaningful life has to have a passion, something or somethings that engage or move one. On the other hand, that something or somethings cannot be solely personal. It must be recognized to have a greater significance than just being the object of a passion. It must be worth being the object of a passion. As she sums it up, "meaning in life consists in and arises from actively engaging in projects of worth. On this conception, meaning in life arises when subjective attraction meets objective attractiveness, and one is able to do something about it or with it."[26]

In Wolf's view, meaningfulness cannot come from either side individually, only from their convergence. If meaning were purely a subjective matter, defined solely by the one's passion, then trivial pursuits, as long as they were deeply felt, could be passionate. Wolf asks us to imagine the case of Sisyphus, who was condemned by the gods to push a rock up a mountain eternally only to watch it roll back down the mountain when he reached the summit. Suppose he were to come to feel a sense of fulfillment in his fate. Would this make his life more meaningful? She suggests that it wouldn't. Rather, it would be a sign of resignation to the meaningless of his existence. (By contrast, Albert Camus' *The Myth of Sisyphus* argues that Sisyphus' engaging in his fate with passion might display the personal strength of embracing the absurdity of an existence that is the fate of all of us.) In order for a life to have meaning it must participate in activities that are actually worthwhile.

On the other hand, that participation does not by itself guarantee meaningfulness. I might be involved in a project of great value, say building a sewage treatment plant in an impoverished area ridden with cholera, and yet feel alienated from my work. This could be for any number of reasons: chronic depression, feeling out of place, thinking that my real vocation is really to be a writer, or others. Unless I am emotionally engaged with the project, unless it feels significant to my own life, it should not be thought of as meaningful in the sense Wolf describes. This may be puzzling to some people for whom a worthy project would seem necessarily to be meaningful. However, Wolf distinguishes between moral worth and meaningfulness. A project may be morally worthy in itself. It may, for instance, be important that I stay involved in building the sewage treatment plant. Perhaps I am the engineer for the plant and there is no one to replace me. We might say in this instance that it is my duty or my obligation to remain involved. This does not mean, however, that it would be meaningful for me to do so. Wolf wants to say that the meaningfulness of a life can be distinguished from its goodness. People can live in all kinds of upstanding ways from which they feel themselves estranged. Goodness and meaningfulness are not necessary companions in human existence.

One might raise questions as to the adequacy of this view of meaning.[27] For our purposes, however, we might accept that meaningfulness has something to do with both the subjective and objective factors she discusses in order to ask whether this enlightens us about the place of deep friendships in our lives. I believe the answer here is yes, for several reasons. First, close friendships do seem to fit the model she lays out for meaningfulness. From the side of objectivity, friendships are generally considered to be an important good in a human life. A life without any close friendships would, for most of us, be impoverished in an important way. This is not to deny that there might be people who can live meaningful lives without them. But, in an Aristotelian turn of phrase, "in general and for the most part" people consider the having of deep friendships a significant element of most human lives.

From the subjective side, deep friendships are clearly aspects of lives that bring them a sense of fulfillment. The liking of a friend, the engagement in shared activities, the conversation: these lend a vibrancy to living of the kind Wolf describes as necessary for meaningfulness. They light up lives. We know what it is like to be immersed in a good talk with a deep friend or to be in the afterglow of an common project with someone we care about. And even in our more pedestrian activities with friends, the sharing of those activities allows them to rise above many of the more mundane tasks that often consume our daily existence.

Following the lead of the subjective side of meaningfulness, there is a second way in which Wolf's approach helps us understand close friendships. She discusses meaning in terms of personal significance, but not in terms of happiness. We have already distinguished happiness of the kind offered by neoliberal consumerism from meaningfulness. Wolf herself distinguishes the subjective side of meaningfulness from happiness. She writes, "someone whose life is fulfilling has no guarantee of being happy in the conventional sense of that term. Many of the things that grip or engage us make us vulnerable to pain, disappointment, and stress. Consider, for example, writing a book, training for a triathlon, campaigning for a political candidate, caring for an ailing friend."[28]

Fulfillment can be distinguished from happiness "in the conventional sense" because the former permeates more deeply into a life than the latter. It is worth noting that all the examples Wolf provides in the quote above involve active engagement. People do not receive fulfillment; they create it, or at least create the conditions for it through their activity. This is in contrast to the passive reception of happiness or pleasure that we have seen in the figure of the consumer. To be subjectively fulfilled in Wolf's sense is not necessarily to be happy—at least in many of the senses of that term. Rather, it is to feel one's life to be worthwhile. This is what it is to be in a close friendship. Close friendships, to be sure, often bring happiness. But their more essential character lies in their bringing fulfillment. If deep friendships were simply a matter of "conventional" or neoliberal happiness, they would be more like social than communicating friendships. Close friendships require not only enjoyment; they also require the undergoing of the lives of others, in their difficulties—and even at times their tragedies—as well as their joys. What gave depth to the trilateral friendship we considered above was the sharing, and indeed effort, it involved for each of the friends to maintain the level of personal connection to sustain those friendships through the dark or uncertain periods. This effort, and the sense of a friendship that arises through it, is captured in Wolf's discussion of the subjective side of meaningfulness.

There is another aspect to this subjective side, one that Wolf does not describe but that allows itself to be drawn from what she does say. It is an aspect we can only gesture at here, but it reveals another way that deep friendships contribute to the meaningfulness of a life. When people look at their lives, they often characterize them in a narrative way. One often recounts one's life to oneself as a story, or as several intersecting stories. In these stories, the worthwhileness of one's life emerges for one.[29] In fact, it is sometimes through the construction of the story that one's life either comes to seem worthwhile or that one lends worthwhileness to it. I tell myself who I am and what I am about through the stories in which I place myself. For example, I am a philosophy professor who used to be a student of psychology. I came to psychology with the thought that I would be able to help people. When I began to study Foucault, however, I became convinced that as a therapist I would not be helping people so much a reinforcing the hold a problematic society had on them. This led me to want to think more about society and politics, which in turn led me to study philosophy. My writings, including this one, have often attempted to reflect upon how we might live in the contemporary world with its particular power arrangements. This narrative, short as it is, displays the kind of story one might tell oneself in thinking about the meaning of one's life. It gives both a coherence and a justification to one of the trajectories my life has followed. That is the point of the life narratives we tell ourselves.

In these narratives, the past has an important role to play. The little story I have just told displays this. Narratives, after all, unfold over a chronological period. They give meaning to the present in part through the way in which it was arrived at. To think about oneself narratively is to enlighten the present by means of the past, and conversely to give the past its coherence in leading to the particular present at which one has arrived.

The importance of narratives for the sense of meaningfulness our lives possess makes our deep friendships inextricable from that sense. Our closest friendships extend into the past to a greater or lesser degree. In telling ourselves who we are, we often refer to those friendships as part of the web of meaningfulness of our lives. Moreover, it is not only the existence of these friends that contributes to a narrative sense of meaning. They contribute to it in two other ways as well. First, they are part of the activities that constitute the narrative. If I were to expand the story of my engagement in philosophy beyond the few sentences I offered a couple of paragraphs ago, a couple of my deep friendships would inevitably appear. I share my past with my close friends, and so they become part of my narratives. Second, those friends do not only appear, they also help shape the character of the narrative itself. We can see this when we recall the importance of communication in deep friendships and Brewer's appeal to self-affirming evaluative outlooks. Deep friends do not only accompany us in the unfolding of our stories; they also help forge those stories. The kind of story I tell myself is partly a product of the close friendships one has had over the years.

The narrative element of the meaningfulness of a life can be seen as an extension of Wolf's discussion of the subjective side of meaning. The stories one tells oneself are part of the vision one has of one's own engagement in life. They may, and often do, reflect values that one might call objective, or at least intersubjective. However, their force lies in the way they situate us in relation to what we do, the way they intersect with, give coherence to, justify, and reinforce the passion with which we do what we do. One way to think of alienation is as a dislocation between one's narrative and one's current activities. Alternatively, to feel "ful-filled" in the sense Wolf uses the term is to be immersed in one's life in accordance with the kind of narrative one tells oneself—or would tell oneself—about who one is and how one got there. In this narrative, or better these narratives (because we rarely tell ourselves only one story about our lives' trajectories), deep friendships play a central role. They accompany and help constitute the trajectory that that narrative takes.

In a recent book, *Rethinking Friendship*, the sociologists Liz Spencer and Ray Pahl try to show the ways in which various kinds of personal connection are alive and well in our society. One of their targets in this investigation is Robert Putnam's influential *Bowling Alone*, which argues that in contemporary society we have become more alone and alienated from one another, as typified in the decline of bowling leagues. (Another of their targets is Zygmunt Bauman, whose work we discussed in the previous chapter.) Spencer and Pahl argue, in accordance with the subti-tle of their book "Hidden Solidarities Revealed" that contemporary soci-eties offer a rich network of social relationships that people participate in. These networks are characterized by an array of friendships, from the superficial to the deeper. In their study of particular communities, "we find that both friend-like and friend-enveloped personal communities contain more friends than family and, in friend-like personal commu-nities, some very important friends are placed in the centre of people's maps."[30] Their argument is that when one turns away from a broad brushstroke approach that focuses on phenomena like organizational membership and toward a study of on-the-ground relationships, one finds a multitude of social relationships, including friend relationships, that belie the evidence of impoverished interpersonal bonds. "The more we explore in detail the range and quality of people's actual rather than imputed social relationships, the more the intricacy of their micro-social worlds—and the hidden solidarities they contain—are revealed."[31]

The argument of this chapter has been in accordance with at least some of what Spencer and Pahl claim. There are various kinds of friend-ships that bring us together in various kinds of ways. To say that each of us is entirely alone or alienated in the neoliberal context would be to ignore the texture of some of our most significant relationships.

On the other hand, the existence of social relationships, even friend relationships, does not entail the existence of significant personal bonds. In consumerist and entrepreneurial friendships people develop relation-ships to each other and one another, but those relationships retain the individualism characteristic of the neoliberal context and its figures. Con-sumerist and entrepreneurial friendships are interpersonal without being personal. Spencer and Pahl's approach is open to this possibility, since they recognize different kinds of friendship relationships. But if we are to retain an awareness of where we are in our current situation, we must not lose sight of the kinds of relationships we are often encouraged to make and to cultivate.

We might say that the deep friendships we have discussed here run counter to the neoliberal context, and as such offer a challenge to it. Conversely, we can worry that that context threatens the character and integrity of those friendships. So far, we have only discussed friendship itself in several of its forms. What remains is to ask about the fate of friendships, particularly deep or close friendships, in a neoliberal period whose themes and figures they oppose.

NOTES

1. Cicero, "On Friendship," in Pakaluk, *Other Selves*, p. 90.
2. Telfer, "Friendship," p. 253.
3. Telfer, "Friendship," p. 253.
4. Telfer insists that we can distinguish the desire for a friend's company from love or infatuation by giving reasons for the former that we might not be able to give for the latter. These reasons involve liking and a sense of a bond with someone. I am a bit skeptical that we can make such analytic distinctions. We should note, however, that, given the non-cognitive character of liking, even if one can offer liking as a reason for the desire for company, that liking itself, since it is for the whole person, is a vague sort of reason.
5. Telfer, "Friendship," p. 252.
6. Little, Graham, *Friendship: Being Ourselves with Others* (Melbourne: Scribe Publications: 2000), p. 14.
7. Little, *Friendship*, p. 76.
8. Little, *Friendship*, pp. 77–78.
9. Little, *Friendship*, p. 78.
10. Little, *Friendship*, p. 14.
11. Little, *Friendship*, p. 14.
12. Little, *Friendship*, p. 15.
13. Brewer, Talbot, *The Retrieval of Ethics* (Oxford: Oxford University Press, 2009), p. 244.
14. Brewer, *The Retrieval of Ethics*, p. 244.
15. Brewer, *The Retrieval of Ethics*, p. 244.
16. Brewer, *The Retrieval of Ethics*, p. 253.
17. Little, *Friendship*, p. 141.
18. Little, *Friendship*, p. 15.
19. Hinchman, "Telling as Inviting to Trust," p. 566.
20. Little, *Friendship*, p. 15.
21. Grau, Christopher, "Love and History," *The Southern Journal of Philosophy*, Vol. 48, No. 3, pp. 264–65.
22. Brewer, *The Retrieval of Ethics*, p. 262. This is also a point Grau insists on particularly in "Irreplaceability and Unique Value," *Philosophical Topics*, Vol 1 and 2, 2004.
23. Bauman, *Liquid Love*, p. 49.
24. Brewer, *The Retrieval of Ethics*, p. 264.
25. I owe this point to conversation with Dick Bernstein, who (rightly) pressed me on it.
26. Wolf, Susan, *Meaning in Life and Why it Matters* (Princeton: Princeton University Press, 2010), p. 26.
27. In *Meaning in Life and Why it Matters*, there are a series of responses, along with Wolf's replies, to her view, not all of which are sympathetic to it.
28. Wolf, *Meaning in Life*, p. 14.

29. For an interesting discussion of this issue, particularly with regard to Wolf's work, see Kauppinen, Antti, "Meaningfulness and Time," *Philosophy and Phenomenological Research*, forthcoming.

30. Spencer, Liz, and Pahl, Ray, *Rethinking Friendship: Hidden Solidarities Revealed* (Princeton: Princeton University Press, 2006), p. 197.

31. Spencer and Pahl, *Rethinking Friendship*, p. 191.

SIX

Friendship as Alternative to Neoliberalism

When I was seventeen I was operated on for a herniated disc. I was told that I was the youngest person in the history of New York Hospital to have such an operation. At that time, the surgery was considered a major one; nothing life threatening, but with a long recovery time. I spent two weeks in the hospital. (I am told that my operation is now done on an out-patient basis, and that people are advised to have someone drive them home from the procedure.) On the first day after the operation, I was encouraged to try to stand, with the assistance of a nurse. I couldn't. I had to be lifted back onto the bed. I suspect that my inability to stand had less to do with any weakness in my back and more to do with the painkillers in my system, which had me fading in and out of consciousness.

Mostly I slept. But once when I awoke there was a friend of mine sitting in a chair across from the bed. He was a fellow runner from the high school cross-country team I had been on before my back injury a year before, but also someone I spent a lot of time with outside of school. I don't remember much about his visit. We may have spoken, but if so I surely didn't say much. What I recall of the visit was awakening several times to find him sitting there, as though patiently waiting for. . . well, for nothing. He was there simply to be with me after an operation that officially ended my high school running career.

Ours was a deep friendship, and continues to be so nearly forty years after that morning (or was it afternoon?) in New York Hospital. And, as with many moments of our friendship, one of us was there for the other because that was what was called for. There was nothing in particular for my friend to gain from his visit—surely not stimulating conversation. His cultivation of the friendship at that moment, as at others, lay in attending

107

to it, or perhaps better in tending to it as one tends to one's garden. The tending will make it grow, to be sure, but for serious gardeners (or so I understand) it is the act of cultivating rather than the eventual produce that calls one among the plants. My friend took a bus from across town to sit by my hospital bedside without hope of conversation or much of anything in the way of human interaction because that was what was to be done.

The previous two chapters addressed itself to a number of characteristics of friendship in general and deep friendships in particular. In this chapter we will look at the ways in which deep friendships are alternatives to the relationships encouraged by neoliberalism and in the next chapter how certain themes among those friendships can lay the foundation for an active resistance to neoliberalism. Several aspects of friendship as an alternative to neoliberalism have already been gestured at. Here we will develop those ideas more specifically in contrast to the figures and relationships of neoliberalism. In the case of my friend sitting at my hospital bedside we can see one of them clearly: the non-economic character of close friendships.

Neoliberal relationships are economic ones. They are centered on consumption and investment. As I was outlining this chapter in a café, I heard a couple conversing behind me. The man was explaining to the woman that all relationships are "transactional." People get involved with other people because they have something to gain by it. Rather than lamenting this fact, he said that one just has to recognize it and "play the game." One must make relationships work for one's own "profit." Aside from the fact that, given that I was outlining this chapter as he spoke made it an eerie moment, it illustrated how much the idea of gain and loss has seeped into our approach to relationships with one another. Whether the gain be instantaneous consumption or future return, we are encouraged to look upon one another in economic terms. We are accountants in our relationships.

Deep friendships cut against the grain of neoliberal relationships. They largely ignore accounting. As we will see, this ignoring is not total, but it is substantial. In cultivating a close friendship we do not calculate gains and losses and we are not focused on the pleasures of the moment. Our activities are dictated by the flow of the relationship itself, by the bends in the river carved by its particular passage through the landscape of our lives. This is how my friend treated our friendship when he visited me at the hospital. It is how we act toward those friends with whom we feel a particularly close bond.

We might say that friendships are more nearly founded on gift-giving than on any kind of economy. There is an entire literature on the role of the gift in certain societies, perhaps the most seminal of which is Marcel Mauss' 1950 essay *The Gift*.[1] Sometimes, when this role is institutionalized into society, it is referred to as a "gift economy," a phenomenon of which Mauss offers several examples. There are rules or at least understood norms for the giving of gifts: how and when they are given, under what conditions, etc. It would not be mistaken to see elements of this economy among the giving that occurs between friends. However, the norms for this "economy" are more specific to the friendships themselves than to a wider set of social norms. Among certain friends it may be the norm to be lavish with each other or one another; among others there may be an ethic of material frugality. And among close friends, there often emerges a norm that jettisons accounting altogether. What I want to stress with the term *gift* is this last type of norm.

To give a gift in this sense is to offer without expectation of return. A gift is a one-off. When my friend visited me in the hospital, his visit was not motivated by I might do for him later. Instead he was doing what he thought might be good for me at that moment. We could also, and perhaps more urgently, see the same idea of the gift in a more fraught moment in the relationship among close friends. There are times in which a friend's evaluative outlook (in Brewer's sense) might need to be challenged. She is not seeing things aright, and as a result feels herself to be a victim or entitled to some vengeance against another or is likely to quit a job or walk away from a love relationship. One feels the need to intervene at this moment out of a sense of loyalty or duty to the friend. This sense of loyalty or duty is more than a matter of general moral obligation. If there were no friendship, the duty would not exist. What is shared with the sense of general moral obligation is the feeling that this intervention will be onerous. It will cause some tension with the friend, even in the context of trust, and one would really rather not do it.

One does it, however, because it is clear the friend requires it. Her life is about to take a wrong turn, so one steps in. One need not take over her life, only confront her with the deficiency in her evaluative outlook that has led her to this pass. The reward for doing this, if it can be called that, would only be to see that the friend's life righting itself.

We might say of these instances of friendship that the context of the friendship allows these particular kinds of gifts to be offered. But this would not be exactly right. In the example of confronting a friend's evaluative outlook, the discomfort it involves indicates that the idea of the friendship "allowing" it is not entirely accurate. Perhaps this kind of confrontation has not occurred before in the history of the friendship. It presents itself as at once necessary and unprecedented. When this happens, the gift of intervention does not follow the previous context of the relationship, but adds a dimension to it. The context of the friendship is changed. The friendship grows, admitting of new possibilities that had previously not existed. This previous non-existence was not a matter of foreclosure. It was not that such confrontation was implicitly forbidden. Rather, the context of the relationship before this confrontation had not been structured by such an interaction nor perhaps even by its possibility.

What is true of this imagined confrontation could be just as true of the hospital visit. It might have been (here my memory is a bit fuzzy) that there was no precedent for such a visit in my previous relationship with my friend. Let's imagine that there wasn't. By visiting me in this way, then, my friend would be opening a new dimension of the relationship, adding a bit of territory to its current map. Unlike the example of the confrontation of an evaluative outlook, this addition was probably not so onerous. It involved taking a crosstown bus and sitting quietly alongside a friend who was in a morphine-induced stupor. (Since this was the 1970s, hanging out with a friend who was in a drug-induced stupor would not, on its own, have been a novel activity.) In offering this gift of the visit the possibility of further gifts like this was also opened up. The gift-giving in a friendship does not only occur within the context of the friendship, then, but can in turn also be determinative for the evolution of that friendship's character.

In seeking to elucidate the non-economic character of deep friendships, we have appealed to the concept of the gift. However, there is an objection the philosopher Derrida raises to the idea that gift-giving eludes an economic structure. If he is right, this objection bears not only on gift-giving itself, but upon the possibility of friendship surmounting neoliberal economics. There is no such thing, in Derrida's view, as a giving that lies beyond the economy of investment and return. *"At the limit,"* he writes, *"the gift as gift* ought *not appear as a gift: either to the donee or to the donor. It cannot be gift as gift except by not being present as gift. . . The temporalization of time. . . always sets in motion the process of a destruction of the gift: through keeping, restitution, reproduction, the anticipatory expectation or apprehension that grasps or comprehends in advance."*[2] The problem of placing the gift outside of all economies, Derrida claims, is that it cannot be given without the knowledge that it is given, which brings with it the expectation of gratitude or return, in the recipient if not in the donor.

We can follow his thought here. If I give you a gift, and you know it is I who gave you this gift, you necessarily feel a debt of gratitude toward me. You can pay this debt in any number of ways. You can give me a gift in return. You can offer me a more generalized gratitude. You can try to match my gift with a better one. You can remain with a sense of undischarged debt. In none of these cases have you escaped the economy of investment and return. The only way to escape them would be if you didn't know the source of the gift, and even then you might feel a puzzled source of gratitude if you knew it was a gift. So the gift cannot even appear as a gift if it is really to be one. The character of gift-giving, then, "always sets on motion the destruction of the gift."

The stakes of this objection are high. If friendship cannot escape the economy of investment and return, then, to one extent or another, the character of entrepreneurial friendships are more than friendships of a given time period. The entrepreneurial character of friendship would be inescapable. It would be at least part of the underlying structure of *all* friendships. There would be no friend that, in giving to another, would not already have involved herself in the economy of debt and return. Even friendships of pleasure, neoliberal consumer friendships, would contain an element of the economic; there would be no partaking of pleasure that did not involve a debt to the source of that pleasure.

In casting the matter this way, however, Derrida removes the gift from the context of friendship within which it arises. Thought of outside the context of a friendship, a gift, whether physical or of some other kind—a giving or an offering to another—may seem to be caught within an economy of investment and return. But in the parameters of certain kinds of friendships this kind of giving can come to make sense. Friendship can develop an interpersonal realm in which the economy of gift and return begins to lose its grip. There is a difference between thinking that a friend will look after one because that person is one's friend and giving to the friend in a particular circumstance *because* that will foster the friend's looking after one. And, from the other side, the gratitude one feels in receiving a friend's gift need not be the payment of a debt. It can, instead, be the joy in inhabiting a relationship that is not reducible to an economy of debts.

How might this come to be? Our first clue would be to look at the role of the past in friendships. If Derrida misses the context in which the gift-giving of friends takes place (and bear in mind here that the gifts we are talking about are rarely material—they are usually matters of time, concern, and involvement), it is because he misses the thickness of the past that underlies the giving of any particular gift. This thickness consists in cooperative activities and in engaged time that form the ether of the friendship. The gifts that friends give each other do not come out of nowhere. They emerge from this ether, an ether that suffuses the friendships in such a way that accounting becomes largely irrelevant.

Of course, the term "largely" in the previous sentence flags a reservation. There are limits to the gift-giving of friendship. In particular, if one friend is always on the giving side and the other always on the receiving one, this will debilitate the friendship. This was a point the philosopher Immanuel Kant saw. In a reflection on friendship, he writes that, "The relationship of friendship is a relation of equality. A friend who bears my losses becomes my benefactor and puts me in his debt. I feel shy in his presence and cannot look him boldly in the face. The true relationship of friendship is cancelled and friendship ceases."[3] From the side of the benefactor, to be always the bearer of gifts is likely to lead to resentment. What parades as a friendship begins to feel like a cover for something more exploitative. In deep friendships, gifts may not be counted, but to one extent or another they come from both sides.

One might object, however, that this caveat gives the game away. They might say that the significance of "largely" is not to indicate the limits of the non-economic character of close friendships but their underlying bent toward the economic. If it cannot be that the one friend always gives and the other always receives, isn't this because there is a silent accounting in friendship, a balance sheet that both are aware of and that both ensure does not enter too much on one side of the ledger? If this is right, then so is Derrida's view of the gift, at least as it applies to friendship.

In order to answer this objection, we must distinguish two possibilities. One is the infusion of friendship with the themes of neoliberalism, especially that of the figure of the entrepreneur. Inasmuch as we are not immune from the influence of our times, we are likely to have some accounting going on in any relationship to the extent that we have taken up the investor stance of neoliberal entrepreneurship. This is likely to be true, and may have some deleterious effect on the friendship itself. It is a point to which we return at the end of this chapter and briefly in the next. However, the current objection wants to cut deeper than that. It asks whether it is of the very nature of a friendship to be economically oriented. Regardless of the conditions under which they take place, are the relationships we have called deep or close friendships necessarily suffused with an economic character of giving and receiving in the way Derrida suggests is part of the very structure of gift-giving?

They are not. It is one thing to say that friendships decline when all of the giving falls to one side and all of the receiving to another. However, it is quite another to say that friends always have their eye on the balance of giving and receiving. When that balance comes into view, it is because there is a problem or at least a perceived problem in the friendship. If I begin to think of a friend as someone I am always giving to, if that idea becomes salient for me, it is because there is a hitch in the relationship. It may not be that the hitch lies in my always being the one giving. It could be, for example, that I have a parent in decline to whom I have had to devote a lot of energy and at the same time my friend is going through a rough patch and I find myself giving to her as well. If I took the longer view, I would see that I am not always giving to her, but, under stress, I feel enervated by her current difficulties. Alternatively, however, it could in fact be that my role with the friend has slipped into that of what Kant calls the "benefactor." In either case, the emergence of a balance sheet into reflective awareness for me is not the indicator of an ongoing underlying economic quality to the friendship, but instead of a problem or at least a perceived problem with its current state.

To see this point, consider going to a movie. If the movie is a good one, you're not aware of the time going by. You're absorbed by the movie, taken in by its plot or its characters or its camera work. The fact that it is an hour and a half long or so doesn't really matter. That is irrelevant to your experience. It is only when the movie is not absorbing that the passage of time begins to matter. You look at your watch and become aware of the moments, one after another. Otherwise, the experience is just about the movie. Now one might want so say that whether or not one is aware of the time passing by, it is passing nevertheless. Just so, there is a silent accounting going on in friendships, whether or not one is noticing it. But this would miss the point of the analogy. In a close friendship there is gift-giving going on without much awareness that it is happening, without each friend saying, "I'm now giving a gift from my side." That is, there is gift-giving without any kind of accounting. It is only when one begins to take account of the giving that there is a problem. Gifts are passed to each other or one another in friendship as time passes in an engrossing movie. In each case, the absorption in what is happening precludes any accounting of that passing. When that accounting happens, it is because there is a problem.

One might go even further in responding to Derrida's economic account of the gift. It is precisely the economic thinking displayed by Derrida's account that converges with neoliberalism, and especially with the figure of the entrepreneur. His discussion of the gift is not a revelation of the gift's inescapably economic nature, but instead a historically situated view (originally published in French in 1991) that is too clearly in keeping with the tenor of the time. Although one might argue that the structure of Derrida's thought of the gift is continuous with his much earlier deconstructive reflections, and therefore not a product of the influence of neoliberalism, one must wonder why, during the rise of neolibealism, he saw a phenomenon as alternative to neoliberal thinking as the gift to be a worthy object of deconstructive reflection.

What grounds the non-economic character of friendship? Why does it display this structure, one that does not actually resist accounting but, in its very nature, seems to run wide of it? We already have the answer before us. It is the trust involved in deep friendships. In neoliberalism there is no room for trust, because neoliberalism pictures people as isolated individuals who occasionally come in contact with each other or one another. In the previous chapter, we saw that this picture does not even accommodate the trust involved in telling. The relationship of telling requires a dependency of one person upon another for the truth of what is told. This dependency, this interpersonal bond, is a relationship for which the neoliberal picture of relationships—and in particular consumerist and entrepreneurial friendships—leaves no room. (We also saw that this does not mean that all of our consumer and entrepreneurial relationships are entirely without the bond of trust—but this is because they are not entirely consumerist or entrepreneurial.) In close friendships, this trust, and the bond which creates it and out of which it is created, is a central element of the relationship between the friends.

Trust allows a deep friendship to run wide of an economic orientation because of the mutual dependency it involves. To depend upon a friend in the way of trust is, as we saw, distinct from having confidence in her in the way of predictability. Trust is not a calculation that the friend will act in certain ways. It is instead a placing oneself in the hands of the friend. It is to let loose (without entirely abandoning) the grip of one's own cognitive orientation toward the world in favor of another's. This letting loose is the jettisoning of the calculation that drives the economic character of neoliberal relationships, and especially entrepreneurial ones. To trust a close friend is not to think that it is likely that she will not lead one astray; it is to be in a space where that thought doesn't arise, because one has put herself at her friend's disposal.

In fact, one might argue that neoliberalism's economic orientation, and its consequent discouragement of trust, helps it reproduce itself. This occurs through a particular dynamic, one that we see in evidence around us. In thinking of others strategically, we isolate ourselves from them through the individualism discussed in earlier chapters. This individualism is reinforced by the loss of economic support characteristic of neoliberal economics. Everyone is on her own, and so everyone is in competition with everyone else. This aloneness breeds a sense of insecurity. In a society in which people were more deeply tied to one another, this insecurity might lead to social solidarity. But in a neoliberal society, where trust is not encouraged, it leads to further distrust of others. This distrust turns one away from others, leading to further individualism and aloneness and greater estrangement from any sense of social solidarity. Distrust breeds distrust, individualism yields greater individualism. Under these conditions, neoliberal practices reproduce themselves easily because there is no social solidarity of the kind we will discuss in the following section to challenge them.

Of course, the depth of trust characteristic of close friendships does not happen with all relationships. It requires the development of a bond between friends that in turn signals the importance of the past in the friendship. Without the past as a ground, it is difficult to imagine friends being able to arrive at a point where they trust each other or one another to the extent of allowing the other's cognitive orientation to be their guide (or, perhaps more precisely, their co-guide). There is a trust in telling that does not require anything more than the minimal dependency of human relationships. But in a deep friendship, where what is at stake is not information but emotional vulnerabilities, fragile hopes, and evaluative outlooks, there has to be a shared ground of the past in order to found the dependency it involves.

This helps us understand the example we discussed some pages back of confronting a close friend's evaluative outlook. The shared past has grounded a relation of trust that has in turn grounded one's ability to confront a friend's failure to see things aright. The dependency in this case does lie not with the person being confronted—or better, it lies with her only secondarily. The primary dependency is that displayed by the confronter. The confronter trusts her friend and their relationship enough to make herself vulnerable by pressing her friend on something the friend is likely to be sensitive about. Confronting evaluative outlooks is not a comfortable affair. People are invested in the way they see the world, and especially in their normative takes on how things ought to be. To confront someone's normative take requires one to trust the strength of the relationship enough to embark on a course of action that is emotionally fraught. It also requires one to abandon all calculation regarding the effect of the confrontation on the relationship. One confronts the friend because that is what is needed, that is what the friend needs. One trusts that this confrontation will be sustainable within the bonds of the friendship, but does not—indeed cannot—be sure exactly what impact it will have upon that friendship.

It might even be argued that a friendship in which this cannot occur, where it is precluded from occurring by the norms of the relationship, is one that is likely not a deep friendship. It would more aptly be called a social friendship, in Little's sense of the term. Social rules are respected; they are not challenged in the name of some more significant communication. If the trust in a friendship has more substance than that of a social friendship, it will admit the kind of dependency that can relinquish the reliance on social norms in order to open the way toward more intimate and sometimes less comfortable interactions. And among those may be interactions whose effect on the friends cannot be calculated in advance, and where the stakes are high enough for one of the friends that those effects ought not even to be considered.

We have referred in passing here to the bond that exists between friends and in particular to its non-individualistic character. This non-individualistic element is also an alternative to neoliberal relationships. In our initial discussion of telling in the fourth chapter, we referred to neoliberal relationships as viewing people like pool balls, occasionally coming into contact but retaining the integrity of their surfaces. The bond between close friends offers a different picture of relationships. It is not the opposite picture, one that has it that friends meld into a single entity. The metaphors of love—that of two becoming one—offer as misleading a picture of friendships as they do of love relationships. Rather, what happens between close friends is that the borders between them become a bit effaced. There remain borders, but they are more porous. There is a rich area of the "between" that goes missing in neoliberal relationships. That is what is meant by the bonds of friendship.

This bond arises from two aspects of the relationship: its trust, rooted in the past of the friendship, and the content of what is shared. We have seen the role trust plays in creating the bond. The communication between close friends, partially based on that trust, places between the friends an array of content that allows each to know the other in ways that those not involved in deep friendships will not. This knowing itself has several aspects. First, there is the information that is shared. This information is not inert. It is not just that one knows facts about her friend. Those facts help create a sense of the friend's orientation, her evaluative outlook as well as her interests and projects. This sense in turns leads toward an empathy with the friend, a feeling toward the friend's life that might be described not as feeling what she feels but perhaps as feeling *alongside* what she feels. This is one way the borders between friends become effaced.

Another lies in a communication that has nothing to do with information. To spend time with a friend, to live with her in Aristotle's sense, is to become accustomed to the way she navigates through the world. Her corporeal style, her emotional reactions, the way she responds viscerally to the world around her: all these are matters first of recognition and then of empathy. When one sees how a friend moves through her life, one can take up that movement, not as one's own but not entirely removed from oneself either. One can begin to predict a friend's likely reaction to one's other friends, getting a sense for instance of whom she would like and whom not. In this way, as well as in the information communicated between them, there are "border crossings" between close friends that do not occur among those neoliberal relationships in which the boundaries of participants are more clearly drawn.

The bonds that structure close friendships lead to yet another way in which such friendships constitute an alternative to neoliberal relationships. We have canvassed this in depth in the previous chapter, so we only need to remind ourselves of it here. In addition to their non-economic character and to their foundation in trust that in turn is founded in bonds that are foreign to the figures of neoliberalism, deep friendships lend meaningfulness to the lives of friends that is distinct from consumer happiness or entrepreneurial profit. We can see this distinction from the angle from which we're currently looking. The bonds between close friends are porous. We not only inhabit our own lives, but can step into the stream of other lives; conversely, others can step into the stream of ours. This implies that, to a greater extent than with those with whom we do not have close relationships, we share both the joys and pains of these friends.

This sharing in its turn has at least two consequences. First, it brings a richness to our lives that is not only the richness of happiness, but that of common experiences. Of course, we do not experience our friends' lives the way they experience them at first hand. Again, the borders between deep friends, while porous, are not effaced. Nevertheless, we are affected by what our friends undergo. This affection is by the totality of their experience, both good and bad. The gain in richness through this sharing is distinct from any gain in happiness that we might have, since it involves both happiness and unhappiness, as well as other feelings and emotions. What our vulnerability to a close friend yields, then, is a spectrum of shared experience that intensifies our lives, offers them a significance they would otherwise lack, but does not necessarily make them happier in the aggregate.

One might want to claim, in entrepreneurial language, that even if we do not become happier through our close friendships, we still profit from them precisely in gaining the significance of shared experience. We can respond to this claim in two ways. First, inasmuch as profit is defined as significance or meaningfulness, the entrepreneurial perspective has given the game away. To achieve this significance requires one to abandon approaching one's relationships in entrepreneurial terms. It requires the diminishing of one's own borders and the abandonment of an orientation toward profit. Second, and from the other side of things, it does not seem to me to be helpful to speak of the achievement of meaningfulness in friendship as a matter of profit. That encourages the kind of approach to friendship that is inimical to its development. Deep friendship cannot be folded into the entrepreneurial figure; to speak as though it can will only encourage the kind of behavior that would be an obstacle to its realization.

The other consequence of this sharing is that it makes us vulnerable to the engagement of our friends. Recall here the example of the person who must confront her friend. To become involved in close friendships is to open the door to having one's evaluative outlook inspected and perhaps criticized by another. It is to put one's closely held, and perhaps not entirely proudly held, engagement with aspects of the world on the table for inspection. This is not because one seeks to do so. It is not as though friendships involve some sort of "judgment time" in which each friend lays out her normative perspective for the other's (or others') assessment. Rather, the porousness of the borders between friends renders this an ongoing possibility. It is because the friend gets to know me in a more intimate way than others, coupled with the responsibility the close friend feels for my welfare, that the friend may touch upon aspects of my emotions or my evaluative outlook that amplify the significance of my life without necessarily adding to its happiness. It may be, and it is fortunate when, this amplification ultimately leads to some degree of happiness as well. But it is not necessary that it do so, as for instance when a friend convinces me that I have been too judgmental of someone I don't like, which requires me to revisit my treatment of them in order to act consistent with my values but not with my desires.

The non-economic character of deep friendship, its trust and its bond, and the kind of meaningfulness it brings are all in contrast to the neoliberal relationships we are encouraged to cultivate. One might think that this provides a haven from neoliberalism, that friendship opens a space that is immune to the dominance of pleasure or investment. On this thought, friendship would be an escape from the influence of our times. However, this cannot be. It is a mistake to think of friendship as lying outside the boundaries of neoliberal influence, as it is a mistake to think of any interpersonal—or for that matter personal—phenomenon as divorced from the influences of the world in which it takes place. Friendships don't arise, and they aren't sustained, in an environment sealed off from the neoliberal world. They are an alternative to neoliberalism and its figures, to be sure, but an alternative that exists within neoliberalism.

We might expect, then, that neoliberalism would push back against deep friendships. This is not because of any perceived threat by neoliberalism. To think in terms of such a threat would be to ascribe an anthropomorphic character to the neoliberal thematic. Neoliberalism is a set of themes and motifs that are privileged in our world, not a person who dominates it. This does not mean that nothing in deep friendship threatens neoliberalism. In fact, as we will see in the next section, there are themes in friendship that can indeed set the stage for a more active confrontation with neoliberal social, economic, and political arrangements. However, that confrontation would not be with neoliberalism per se, but rather with institutions and practices that constitute and sustain it. And, in any event, the alternative character of friendship we are currently discussing, if it challenges the themes of neoliberalism, does so not through confrontation but simply through being the kind of friendship it is.

Concommitantly, the push-back from neoliberalism lies simply in neoliberalism being what *it* is. Neoliberal themes infiltrate our lives. We are not sheltered from their influence. To live in a neoliberal world is to be encouraged to think of one's fellows in terms of pleasure and profit. It is to be encouraged to be consumers and entrepreneurs. We saw in the first chapter that Michel Foucault taught us that power is productive, that it does not just prevent people from being or doing certain things but actually molds them in a constitutive way. The figures of the consumer and the entrepreneur are not outside of us. To one extent or another, they *are* us. And because we are encouraged to become neoliberal figures, and because we cannot wholly resist the dominant themes of our times, to one extent or another who we become and how we relate to each other and to one another is partly determined by neoliberal themes. This is the push-back from neoliberalism against deep friendship: not its resistance to such friendship but the effects of its pervasiveness in molding us into beings for whom friendship is motivated by other concerns.

How effective is neoliberalism in molding relationships against the grain of deep friendships? It is a bit difficult to say; however, there is some indirect evidence that it has at least some power to do so. Robert Lane, whose sociological work we have discussed, offers this indirect evidence in his work. He does so almost in spite of himself, in the modifications of his view from an earlier book to a later one. His book *The Market Experience* was published in 1991. There he finds little evidence that the centrality of markets affect friendships in deleterious ways. In discussing friendship, he writes, "The evidence for anything like the commodification of human beings in market economies is slight. The impressionistic observations of historians is contradictory and the more systematic evidence from surveys seems to refute the allegation."[4] Lane bases this conclusion in a survey of various studies. Some suggest that the goods exchanged in the economic realm do not transfer to friendship, which consists in the sharing of non-material goods. "Money can be exchanged where friendship and love cannot. . . Therefore, what people learn about the uses of money cannot easily be transferred to friendship or love relationships."[5] Economic relations are exchange relations, while friendship does not involve exchange. Since they are oriented differently, there is at least an obstacle for commodification to overcome if it is to infect friendship relationships.

More pointedly, "A detailed study of people's beliefs about themselves, their social roles and life concerns, shows a shift between 1957 and 1976 toward a greater attention to and a higher evaluation of personal intimacy and more concern with personal relationships, as contrasted to an emphasis on relatively impersonal status and relationships earlier. . . There is, therefore, reason to doubt the range and depth of the phenomena alleged to be characteristic of modern societies."[6] This result, if accurate, would cast doubt upon the idea that the market economy, at least in the years under study, would have undermined friendship relationships. In fact, things seem to point in the opposite direction.

It is worth recognizing the years covered by the study. It starts in 1957 and ends in 1976. We can make two remarks about these years. The study ends in the wake of the upheavals of the late 1960s and early 1970s. One might expect that those years would indeed have led to a greater emphasis on personal relationships. Among the complaints of the generation of the 60s against society was an alienating commodification, one that stultified human relationships. The finding that people valued those relationships more in the mid-70s than in the late 50s should not be surprising; it might even be expected.

The other remark is that 1976 is at the beginning of the period of neoliberalism. It is only a few years after the Arab oil embargo, three years before the election of Margaret Thatcher, and four years before the election of Ronald Reagan. If neoliberalism threatens the character of personal relationships, one would expect those effects after rather than before 1976. And, in a later book, aptly entitled *The Loss of Happiness in Market Democracies*, Lane finds evidence precisely for this. As with his earlier book, the studies he canvasses are—as he recognizes—suggestive rather than compelling. But what they suggest is a change from an earlier focus on personal relationships and intimacy. Lane does not revise his idea that commodification does not directly undercut friendship, at least in the sense that an emphasis on consumption "crowds out" the cultivation of friends. However, he does find friendship to be threatened from several quarters. "By these (inadequate) tests, the hypothesis that a 'rage to consume' crowds out socializing fails. If the market has a destructive influence on friendship (and I think it does), it must be, as discussed above, through the elevating of instrumentalist and materialist values over social values, the eroding of communities and neighborhoods, and the intermittent increasing of the demand for overtime labor—as in the mid-1990s."[7] Let us briefly examine each of these in turn.

The elevation of instrumentalist and materialist values is central to the figures of the consumer and the entrepreneur. In denying that the activity of consumption itself crowds out socializing, Lane is only denying that people spend less time socializing because they are spending the time shopping that was previously spent on relationships. (Again, however, the studies he cites end in the mid-1970s to early 1980s.) The figures of neoliberalism, however, are not defined by the amount of time spent in consumption and investment, but in the values of consumption and investment that they embrace. Life in its various aspects is seen through the lenses of pleasure and profit. One can indeed pass many hours alongside others with whom one is shopping (for example, hanging out at the mall) or networking. The salient question is how that time is spent. Is it in developing close friendships or is it instead defined by "instrumentalist and materialist values"? Inasmuch as it is the latter, then we indeed have the figures of the (materialist) consumer and the (instrumentalist) entrepreneur.

The other two elements that have served to undermine friendship, the eroding of communities and the demand for overtime, precede neoliberalism but are likely reinforced by it. The former concerns the mobility of people in contemporary society. People move around to follow their jobs more than they did, say, earlier in the previous century. This mobility creates obstacles to sustaining close friendships, and in particular to the Aristotelian criterion of sharing lives. Regarding overtime, Lane is leery of some studies that claim a steady increase in overtime during the past several decades, but finds a temporary increase in overtime and stress in the mid-1990s. He also notes in passing another source of stress that has indeed become more prominent since the publication of the his book: "for workers, competition among firms—made worse by globalization—is the enemy."[8] Competition of this kind brings stress to workers, who are constantly in fear of losing their positions to lower-paid workers in another country. Stress in turn is not conducive to focusing on the cultivation of relationships.

For our purposes, it is the first of these elements of "market democracies," instrumentalist and materialist values, that is the most significant.

These are the values embodied in the figure of neoliberalism. Moreover, as Lane discusses, even where there alternative values are recognized, there is still a tendency to act contrary to those values under the pressure of the values endorsed in one's social milieu. He cites a pair of studies that shows a discordance between the ends people value and the means they value that would lead them to these ends. "Among end states, 'taking care of loved ones' comes first, but the qualities that make families successful (loving) are not highly valued. On the other hand, wealth (a comfortable life) is ranked quite low, but the qualities required to attain that wealth (ambition and hard work) are ranked very high... Where the values of ends and means are out of harmony, change is more likely. But if we value the quality of persons more than material wealth and 'ambition' dominates 'loving,' we are likely to move in the wrong direction."[9] Both of these studies cover a period immediately before (the means values study covers 1968–1971) or during the early phase (the ends values study covers 1968–1981) of neoliberalism. However, the wrong direction that Lane is concerned about seems be the one taken, particularly with the ascendance of the consumer and the entrepreneur.

To say that neoliberalism threatens deep friendships should not be cause for despair. First, it is unlikely that such friendships will disappear. Here, as elsewhere, it is a matter of the more and the less. The pressures of neoliberalism and what it seeks to make of us press against the cultivation and sustaining of close friendships. Alongside the various other influences and stresses of contemporary society, it presents obstacles to maintaining this centrally significant aspect of our lives. But this is a two-edged sword. Just as neoliberalism cuts against close friendships, so close friendships cut against neoliberalism. If we seek a place to escape the values and lives on offer in a neoliberal society, we need not look very far. Our friendships provide a space where an alternative to consumerism and investment can be nourished. We need not await a revolutionary change in the structure of our political or economic arrangements in order to escape some of their more deleterious aspects. We can look closer to home, and we can look there here and now. To be immersed in a deep friendship is already to refuse to be overtaken by the values fostered in a neoliberal society. It is to envision an alternative life, one marked by trust, connection, and meaningfulness rather than pleasure or profit.

We might press the issue in a more deeply political direction. We might ask, and indeed we are about to ask, whether friendship can provide tools not only to create an alternative to neoliberal values and lifestyles, but whether it can begin to found active resistance to it. Is there anything in friendship that can be utilized in forming an open challenge to neoliberalism, not only in its values but in its very structure. Here the answer is more complicated. There are certainly elements of friendship that can do so, but they must be prised apart from those that might sap political resistance. Rightly conceived, however, we might look toward some of the themes of deep friendship in order to structure, learn, and motivate resistance to the neoliberal order.

NOTES

1. Mauss, Marcel, *The Gift: The Form and Reason for Exchange in Archaic Societies* tr. W. D. Halls, (New York: W.W. Norton, 1990 [1950])
2. Derrida, Jacques, *Given Time: 1. Counterfeit Money*, tr. Peggy Kamuf, (Chicago: University of Chicago Press, 1992), p. 14.
3. "Lecture on Friendship," in Pakaluk, *Other Selves*, pp. 213–14.
4. Lane, *The Market Experience*, p. 219.
5. Lane, *The Market Experience*, p. 213.
6. Lane, *The Market Experience*, p. 215. The study he cites is Joseph Veroff, Elizabeth Douvan, and Richard A. Kalka, *The Inner Americans: A Self-Portrait from 1957 to 1976* (New York: Basic Books, 1981).
7. Lane, *The Loss of Happiness in Market Democracies*, p. 188.
8. Lane, *The Loss of Happiness in Market Democracies*, p. 162.
9. Lane, *The Loss of Happiness in Market Democracies*, pp. 92–93. The study of end values Lane cites is Rokeach, Milton, and Ball-Rokeach, Sandra J., "Stability and Change in American Value Priorities, 1968–1981," *American Psychologist*, Vol. 44, 1989, pp. 775–84. The study of means values is Rokeach, Milton, "Change and Stability in American Value Systems: 1968–1971," *Public Opinion Quarterly*, Vol. 38, 1978, pp. 222–38.

SEVEN

Friendship as Resistance to Neoliberalism

In a late interview with Michel Foucault entitled, "Friendship as a Way of Life," Foucault contrasts a more reassuring view of homosexuality as a purely sexual affair with another view, one that is more troubling for contemporary social arrangements. He notes that the more reassuring view "annuls everything that can be uncomfortable in affection, tenderness, friendship, fidelity, camaraderie and companionship, things which our rather sanitized society can't allow a place for without fearing the formation of new alliances and the tying together of unforeseen lines of force."[1] Foucault suggests here that homosexual relationships, in part because they can involve affections that are not able to be monitored or channeled by the policing of contemporary social relationships, are threatening to the social order. Foucault's suggestion is one that we will pursue. However, its pursuit is not limited to homosexual friendship.

There is an entire literature on the relation of friendship to politics. Unsurprising, it often roots itself in Aristotle's discussion of *philia* in the *Nichomachean Ethics*. *Philia*, it will be recalled, refers not only to what we would call friendship but to a wider arena of social relationships, and so might be enlisted for discussions of the ways in which personal relationships relate to political ones. Indeed, Aristotle himself enlists *philia* for these purposes, discussing in his chapter on friendship the bond between *philia* and justice and the role of *philia* in different political constitutions. He notes that, "all associations seem to be parts of the political community, but the kind of friendship prevalent in each will be determined by the kind of association it is."[2]

Contemporary discussion of the relation of friendship to politics often develops these themes. The philosopher Alasdair MacIntyre, for instance, complains that the "notion of the political community as a common project is alien to the modern liberal individualist world. . . we have no conception of such a form of community, concerned, as Aristotle says the *polis* is concerned, with the whole of life, not with this or that good, but with man's good as such. It is no wonder that friendship has been relegated to private life and thereby weakened in comparison to what it once was."[3] The political philosopher Hannah Arendt, an endorser of civic friendship, writes "The political element in friendship is that the truthful dialogue of each of the friends can understand the truth inherent in the other's opinion. . . This kind of understanding—seeing the world (as we say rather tritely today) from the other fellow's point of view—is the political kind of insight par excellence."[4] And political theorist Danielle Allen argues that, "Friendship turns out to be not merely a metaphor for citizenship but its crucial component."[5] This is because in order to preserve a polity one must learn to relate to fellow citizens in an equitable and reciprocal manner.

Our concern here is not with the broader question of how friendship and politics interact. This is not because this interaction is irrelevant to questions of neoliberalism. For instance, it may be that a polity characterized by equity and reciprocity would at least mitigate some of the more deleterious effects of neoliberalism, and would act as a counter to its individualism. We will see these themes in our discussion, but will approach it from a different angle. Rather than canvassing the broader relation of friendship to politics, we will ask, in keeping with the themes developed in the previous chapter, about the relevance of close or deep friendship for a politics of that might resist neoliberal encroachment. This will be a progressive politics of solidarity, one that embraces certain aspects in deep friendships, developing them in the political struggle against neoliberalism. Specifically, we will see that deep friendships can provide certain thematic elements necessary for a politics of solidarity, can prepare one for engagement with it, and can motivate it.

If we are to appeal not just to friendship in general, but to deep or close friendships, our discussion must clear a particular hurdle before we can begin to develop those themes. This hurdle, which has appeared throughout the discussion of friendship, concerns the argument that the intimacy of a close friendship not only does not prepare one for political solidarity but actually stands as an obstacle to it. Friendships of usefulness may, as Aristotle notes, lend themselves to political engagement for the sake of mutual self-interest. Friendships of pleasure, while not necessarily tilting toward political engagement, are not inimical to it either. But deep friendships, because of their particular character, seem to turn one away from political involvement or solidarity. This can be for at least two related reasons: the limited number of deep friendships one can have and the irreplaceability associated with them.

The conflict between the limited number of deep friendships one can have and political engagement, like many other issues in friendship, was addressed by Aristotle. He writes, "Now, in the kind of friendship that exists among fellow citizens, it is actually possible to be friends with many people without being obsequious and while remaining truly a good man. But to be a friend of many people is impossible, if the friendship is to be based on virtue or excellence and on the character of our friends [i.e., Aristotle's true friendship]. We must be content if we find even a few friends of this kind."[6] True friendship does not offer a solid foundation for political relationships. The depth of commitment it involves—the requirement that true friends live together—preclude it from standing as a basis for relationships in a polity. This would seem to be even more emphatically true for a politics of solidarity, i.e., a grassroots movement opposing aspects of neoliberalism. Deep friendships would not stand as way to bring people together, but instead would create internal divisions that would be obstacles to the development of a cohesive political movement.

This sentiment is echoed in the work of the recent philosopher Jacques Derrida in his book *The Politics of Friendship*. There is a tension, in his view, between friendship and a democratic politics that lies in the fact that friendship can only extend to a limited number of people: "it is not possible to love while one is simultaneously, at the same time (*áma*), the friend of numerous others (*to de pollois áma einai phílon kai to phileîn kolúei*); the numerous ones, the numerous others—this means neither number nor multiplicity in general but *too great a number*."[7] Friendship requires spending time and expending emotion on those one befriends; it is impossible to engage in this level of interpersonal concentration with numerous people, especially in the kinds of deep friendship we have sketched here. For a friendship to move beyond the parameters set by the figures of neoliberalism there needs to be a level of involvement that precludes the possibility of drawing the circle of one's friends very wide. As a result, one might see friendship, not as we have suggested here as a support for an egalitarian politics, but rather in tension with it. There must of necessity be an inside and an outside, the inside including those with whom one has been able to construct friendships and the outside consisting in everyone else.

This difficulty drawn here by Aristotle and Derrida is, for our purposes, twofold. First, since one cannot be close friends with a wide array of people, deep or close friendship is an inappropriate model for political solidarity. Second, and more disturbing, there may be a tension between close friendship and political solidarity, a tension that stems from demarcating an inside where one's close friends are and an outside where everyone else is.

Robert Lane sounds similar concerns regarding the tension between the intimacy of a close friendship and the requirements of participation in a democratic polity. In particular, he notes the tension between the affective relations of friends and the rationality necessary for political reflection, between the personal character of friendship and the impersonality of public deliberation, and between the centripetal nature of close friendship and the centrifugal requirements of respect for fellow citizens.[8]

The worry these various passages converge on is that close friendship is not only different from but also and more pointedly inimical to political solidarity and democratic participation. We can articulate this worry from another angle, that of the irreplaceability of friends. We saw in the previous chapter that close friendships are both unique and irreplaceable. They are unique in that they occupy a particular place in a person's life. They are irreplaceable in that that place cannot be replicated by other relationships. This is the source of Montaigne's famous quote, "because it was he; because it was I." This uniqueness and irreplaceability can only be had with those particular friends with whom one has that particular history. As Alexander Nehamas says, "My friends stand out against the rest of the world of my acquaintance and make, to me at least, a difference that counts: they are, to that extent, individuals. Since, when I see my friends in their actions, I depend on our history together and I see something no one else sees, I too am, to that extent, an individual."[9]

The particularity of deep friendships contrasts with the requirements of political solidarity. It creates a bond between friends that is not only a space apart from the space one shares with others, but a space that seems to compete with it. There are those with whom I have devoted relationships that are constitutive of the meaningfulness of my life; and then there are the others. Not only does deep friendship seem to offer an unpromising basis for building movements of political connection; indeed it seems to move us in the opposite direction, toward privacy and exclusiveness.

If we are to be able to claim that deep friendships can have some political resonance, particularly in the way of forming a resistance to neoliberalism, we will have to clear this hurdle. In doing so, we need to get more precise on how this is a difficulty for political organizing and resistance. One could take the above complaints in a strong sense, one that implies that it is impossible at once to be in close friendships and politically involved. The idea here would be that because deep friendship moves us in the opposite direction from politics, people with deep friends, having been so moved, would no longer be in the political arena.

This seems too strong a claim. We all know people who are committed to politics in a variety of ways, from the grassroots solidarity we will be most interested in here to public speaking to working for candidates to running for office, many of whom indeed have close friendships. There seems no bar to having close friendships on the one hand and being politically involved on the other. If there is a problematic relationship between friendship and politics, it cannot be that one cannot have close friendships and still be politically involved.

A slightly weaker claim, one that does seem to capture the worries articulated here, is that there are themes in friendship that are inimical to political involvement. Rather than saying that deep friendships *preclude* political engagement, one might say that deep friendships are *in tension* with such engagement. This tension could be lived in several different ways. For instance, it could be that when one is cultivating a friendship, one cannot simultaneously be politically involved. But even this seems too strong. There are political movements in which close friends participate without either lessening their commitment or compromising their friendship. Alternatively, one could claim that there are particular elements or aspects of friendship that are in tension with political involvement. On this view, if one is to be able to participate adequately in politics, one would have to lay aside these elements of the friendship during the period of that participation. So, for example, two close friends could both participate in politics together, but they would have to leave certain aspects of their friendship unexpressed while they do so.

This is a more plausible interpretation of the concerns expressed by Aristotle, Derrida, and Lane, among others. The limited number of close friends one can have, the intimacy they share, the irreplaceability of each in the other's lives: these all provide obstacles to wider political involvement. Inasmuch as they figure in close friendships, they tend to draw one away from the necessities such involvement requires. Therefore, if one is adequately to participate in politics, one must resist the encroachment of these elements of friendship.

If we situate friendship this way, we can make an important distinction. It is not close friendship per se that is inimical to politics, but rather certain themes within it. But if we put matters like this, we leave open another possibility. While there may be certain themes in friendship that militate against political participation, there may be others that militate in favor of it. That is what I would like to argue. The worries cited by the above authors are real worries. Friendship can turn inward. Because close friendships are situated at the center of meaningfulness for many lives (and recall that we have not precluded love relationships from close friendships), their intimacy and their irreplaceability could indeed draw one away from wider public concerns. But friendship is more thematically rich than that. There are aspects of friendship that can lead one toward political involvement, and especially toward the political involvement we are envisioning here, one that is oriented toward a political solidarity in resistance to neoliberalism. And if we bear in mind that neoliberalism itself is a threat to the character of deep friendship, we can see immediately (and we will return to this) a reason one would want to engage in resistance to neoliberalism.

What themes of deep friendship would contribute to the kind of solidarity characteristic of a political movement that might challenge neoliberalism? We have already seen at a general level an element of friendships that could set the stage for such a challenge in Little's discussion of communicating friends. Communicating friends, in his view, contrast with social and familiar friends in offering support for confronting social norms. Recall his claim that, "Pure friendship is an alternative to society, a platform for criticising it, for social and moral invention and individually chosen lines of self-improvement." Deep friendships, because they allow for reflection on evaluative outlooks, and because they offer safe havens for self-invention, open up a space for reflection on the values of a given social, political, and economic arrangements. And because they do so, they are capable of supporting challenges to these arrangements.

This support is in contrast to the self-reinforcing movement of neoliberalism we discussed in the previous section of this chapter. We noted there that one of the ways neoliberalism reproduces itself is by endorsing an individualism and distrust of others that preclude the formation of social solidarity. This leaves people feeling isolated and alone, which leads them to further distrust, which leads to further individualism, which prevents solidarity. The dynamic of communicating friends moves in the opposite direction. Its intimacy and solidity provide a bulwark against the feelings of aloneness that might accompany a challenge to social norms. With close friends we feel less alone in a world that tells us we are alone, less insecure in a world that breeds insecurity. As a result, we might be more emboldened to confront the values we are asked to embrace, the relationships we are encouraged to form, and the practices we are channeled to participate in.

This aspect of friendship is a general one. There is another aspect, one we have not discussed previously, that even more profoundly contributes to the formation of solidarity movements capable of confronting neoliberalism. It concerns the role that equality plays in close friendships.

The philosopher Immanuel Kant writes that, "The relationship of friendship is a relation of equality. A friend who bears my losses becomes my benefactor and puts me in his debt. I feel shy in his presence and cannot look him boldly in the face. The true relationship of friendship is cancelled and friendship ceases."[10] Kant's argument here is that friendship requires a delicate balance between how much is asked and offered from one friend to another. We discussed this issue above in talking about the limits of the non-economic character of close friendships. However, there is another way to take this citation. Deep friendships are relations of equality. We might amend Kant by saying that they are relations of equality not because of the general balance of giving and receiving but because in many cases that balance does not even come into play. That is to say, I look at my friend as an equal, not because he or she is equal in measure to me but because equality of this type is, to a certain extent, beyond measure. The equality here is an equality of two or more people who take one another not as equals in this or that characteristic but, we might say, as equals, period.

Equality is the basis for a truly democratic politics in many political theories. As the economist and political theorist Amartya Sen has written, "a common characteristic of virtually all the approaches to the ethics of social arrangements that have stood the test of time is to want equality of *something*—something that has an important place in the particular theory."[11] What we are interested in here, however, is in the formation of movements of solidarity that might challenge the neoliberal order. For that purpose, we will turn to the view of recent French theorist Jacques Rancière. I have written more extensively on Rancière elsewhere,[12] and can only offer a brief sketch of his views here, one that, I hope, catches the flavor of his thought and its relevance for political solidarity.

Rancière contrasts what he calls, borrowing from Michel Foucault's lectures at the Collège de France, the term *police* that we saw earlier, with what he calls *politics*. "Politics," he writes, "is generally seen as the set of procedures whereby the aggregation and consent of collectivities is achieved, the organization of powers, the distribution of places and roles, and the systems for legitimizing this distribution. I propose to give this system of distribution another name. I propose to call it *the police*."[13] The police, then, are not the folks in uniforms with truncheons. Rather, the police is broadly the set of hierarchical distributions and their justifications characteristic of a particular society. We do not need to linger over the specifics of this concept, since for our purposes it stands as the background for the more relevant concept of politics, or what I have called democratic politics.

What, then, is politics? "I. . . propose to reserve the term *politics* for an extremely determined activity antagonistic to policing: whatever breaks with the tangible configuration whereby parties and parts or lack of them are defined by a presupposition that, by definition, has no place in that configuration—that of the part that has no part. . . political activity is always a mode of expression that undoes the perceptible divisions of the police order by implementing a basically heterogeneous assumption, that of the part who have no part, an assumption that, at the end of the day, itself demonstrates the contingency of the order, the equality of any speaking being with any other speaking being."[14] This, I grant, is a bit of a mouthful. In order to unpack it, it is worth focusing on the term he uses twice: the part that has no part.

In any police order, there are various hierarchies. These hierarchies often differ in different societies, but it is difficult to find an example of a society without one. There are hierarchies of gender, of race, of sexual orientation, of class, of religion, of age, etc. One of the central functions of these hierarchies is to deny participation, or at least equal participation, to those considered to be on the wrong end of the hierarchy. Putting the matter in different terms, there are those who are considered by a society as having a part to play in its direction and maintenance, and those who do not have a part. In a complex society, such as ours, there is no single

strict division between those who do and do not have a part, but instead
a series of distinct but often overlapping or intersecting divisions. These
divisions can work in two opposing directions at the same time, for example with upper-class women who have a part because of their class
that is often denied because of their gender, but nevertheless they operate
by allocating roles that have to do with, in Rancière's terms, having and
not having a part.

Politics, then, as he defines it, is a matter of members of a part that has
no part in a given police order acting as though they indeed do have a
part, acting as though the police order which has not allocated them a
part is contingent, or better arbitrary, and indeed unjustified. It is a matter of those who do not have a part presupposing that they are equal to
those who do, and acting on the basis of that presupposition. As Rancière
puts the point, they act on the presupposition of the equality of any
speaking being with any other speaking being.

In Rancière's view, then, equality is the basis for any truly democratic
politics. "Political activity," he writes, "is always a mode of expression
that undoes the perceptible divisions of the police order by implementing
a basically heterogeneous assumption. . . the equality of any speaking
being with any other speaking being."[15] What the assumption of equality
accomplishes is to challenge the hierarchical order, what Rancière calls
the *police* order, of most social arrangements. To act democratically is to
act collectively on the presupposition of the equality of anyone and everyone. To do so, as Rancière insists, is to act with a sort of collective trust.
He writes, "The test of democracy must ever be in democracy's own
image: versatile, sporadic—and founded on trust."[16] The suggestion I
want to make here is that modes of friendship that resist the figures of
neoliberalism offer both models of and routes toward such a democratic
politics.

Rancière claims that, "The essence of equality is in fact not so much to
unify as to declassify, to undo the supposed naturalness of orders and
replace it with the controversial figures of division."[17] The supposedly
natural figures of the neoliberal order are the entrepreneur and the consumer. In taking a friendship as without measure in the way we have
described, in seeing friends as those whose own stakes are importantly
our stakes, in resisting the reduction of social relationships to pleasures
or investments, what emerges is precisely a declassification in Rancière's
sense. It is not in the name of something else, unless we want to call that
something else either *equality* or perhaps *solidarity* itself, that the figures
of neoliberalism are challenged. It is instead for a type of relationship
without hierarchy, or with as little hierarchy as our age permits.

What is the movement, or some might fear slippage, between equality
and solidarity that appeared in the previous paragraph? This is crucial,
since it is the thematic overlap between friendship and a politics of resistance to neoliberalism. To treat someone as an equal is to treat her as

someone one acts with, or alongside, but not above or instead of. It is to presuppose that she is capable of forming life plans and enacting them (not alone, of course, but in a social context) instead of having to be told who she should be or who she really is deep inside or how she should think about her life. This does not preclude disagreement among equals. To treat someone as an equal does not require that one treats her as immune to mistakes or errors about herself or others. Instead it is, when one finds an equal to be mistaken, to converse with her about her error, presupposing her to be capable of seeing it or even correcting oneself if one has missed something she has seen. Equality does not foreclose engagement and disagreement, or even conflict. What it forecloses is the presupposition that the person with whom one is in conflict is a lesser being than oneself.

One might wonder how important this presupposition is for politics. It is central in two ways. First, consider the political battles that have been fought over the presupposition of equality. Every civil rights movement, perhaps every human rights movement, has been a struggle over who is considered an equal. The previous century, and still the current one, can be characterized as a century of the politics of equality, from women to darker skin peoples to gays to workers to the disabled. When Rancière calls *all* politics a matter of movements that emerge out of the presupposition of equality, one might call this a hyperbole. However, if it is, it is not by much. Moreover, one might indeed argue that all *democratic* politics is a matter of collective action out of the presupposition of equality.[18]

This leads to the second way in which the presupposition of equality is central for politics. Precisely because these struggles have been for equality and against inequality, they have had to assert the equality of those who are being presupposed as less than equal by the social structure or what Rancière calls the police order. In one way or another, it is equality that has been the stated presupposition of those who have engaged in struggle. And in the best of those struggles, the ones we hold up as exemplars of political struggle, for instance the civil rights movement of the 1960s in the US, not only has the presupposition of equality been declared, it has often been practiced. Think here of the lunch counter sit-ins, the Freedom Rides, the general ethos of nonviolence. These are expressions of equality, expressions that bring to the fore the role of equality in struggles against the inequalities with which our history has been laden.

It would not be an exaggeration to say that solidarity is the collective presupposition of equality, and that action out of solidarity is nothing other than action that emerges from the collective presupposition of equality. And friendship, because it is a relationship among equals, one defined by mutual trust, embodies equality in a way that can be translated to movements of solidarity and against the encroachments of neoliberalism.

Moreover, as Marilyn Friedman points out, the fact that friendship is a "voluntary choice" allows it to act as an egalitarian type of relationship that cuts across the traditional structures of a police order and allows alternative and disruptive communities to form. She notes that, "Because of its basis in voluntary choice, friendship is more likely than many other relationships, such as those of family and neighborhood, to be grounded and sustained by shared interests and values, mutual affection, and possibilities for generating reciprocal respect and esteem," adding that "friendship, more so than many other relationships, can provide social support for people who are idiosyncratic, whose unconventional values and deviant lifestyles make them victims of intolerance from family members and others who are involuntarily related to them."[19] This, she points out, is essential to feminist formations of solidarity, which face steep and often violent resistance to their challenges to traditional sex and gender roles.

One might want to argue here against Friedman that one of the virtues of neoliberalism is that it has undermined traditional gender roles, equalizing everyone in the face of globalized market exchange. Jagdish Bhagwati, whose defense of globalization we mentioned in the first chapter, makes this argument in his *In Defense of Globalization*.[20] He urges, characteristically using anecdotal evidence, that women who receive paid labor, even under difficult conditions, establish both pride and a sense of independence. This contrasts with the unpaid labor they perform in their more traditional roles. This argument, however, is wrong on two counts.

First, women, particularly in less technologically advanced countries, have not so much been liberated from traditional gender roles as shifted from one set of oppressive roles to another. For instance, in many of the export processing zones developed by transnational corporations, women are drawn into exploitative work whose effects are little more than to trade in being at the bottom of a traditional social ladder for being at the bottom of the neoliberal one. (Bhagwati concedes that export processing zones can be exploitative, but seeks to minimize their oppressive character. However, the latter has been amply documented in Naomi Klein's *No Logo*.[21]) David Harvey notes that, "Accumulation by dispossession typically undermines whatever powers women may have had within traditional household production/marketing systems and within traditional social structures and markets. The paths of women's liberation from traditional patriarchal controls in developing countries lie either through degrading factory labour or through trading on sexuality."[22] Second, the promised equality is not the kind of equality that Friedman thinks is the basis of feminist emancipation. What she calls "idiosyncratic" or "deviant" lifestyles do not consist in making money or buying goods (or, in more economically advanced countries, purchasing Goth clothes at Hot Topic). They are, instead, experiments in different forms of non-exploitative personal relationships: as Foucault would have it, friendship as a way of life.

A different but more sympathetic objection would be that the solidarity we have described, one that is rooted in the work of Jacques Rancière, is not a solidarity against neoliberalism in particular, but instead against any kind of oppression. After all, many of the movements of the twentieth century pre-date the rise of neoliberalism. Inasmuch as egalitarian solidarity is characteristic of such movements, would it not be more accurate to say that the equality of friendship is a theme that can be carried into solidarity movements in general, not simply into movements that resist neoliberalism?

It is true that Rancière's depiction of democratic political movements characterize not only movements against neoliberalism but are lessons more broadly applied to the practice of solidarity. We certainly do not want to deny this; in fact, it is one of the virtues of his general account of democratic politics that it is applicable to a wide range of contexts. However, his characterization has particular bearing on political organizing in the context of neoliberalism. This is because the figures of neoliberalism are, as we have seen, extraordinarily individualizing. They move us precisely in the opposite direction from solidarity. Rather than seeing others with whom we share this world as equals, neoliberalism encourages us instead to see them as resources or competitors or objects of entertainment. We are made distant from others, not brought close to them. And inasmuch as we approach others through one of these modes, the collective character of solidarity will elude us. As we will see below, one of the ways in which friendship helps create solidarity is through training to trust others. This training creates the glue that keeps movements of solidarity together. At this moment I am emphasizing the related point that the theme of equality in friendship can lay the groundwork for thinking about solidarity in ways that cut against the individualizing strategies of neoliberalism. This makes friendship's equality relevant not only generally for movements of political resistance, but particularly urgent in the context of neoliberalism.

Because of the individualizing tendency of neoliberalism, we often find it difficult to think in terms of solidarity. I suspect that this is one of the reasons people often feel alone and disconnected in the neoliberal context. We don't possess ways of thinking in terms of solidarity, because we are discouraged from thinking in these ways. I am struck by how many of my students feel that there is something wrong with the world, resonate with discussions like Marx's treatment of alienation, recognize the emptiness of lives of consumption, but insist that there is nothing to be done about it. They feel alone; solidarity is not a possibility they recognize. What friendship, which these students do recognize as a possibility for them, provides is a model that will give us the concept of equality in a way that is relevant for constructing collective resistance to the domination of neoliberalism.

Before we turn to the way in which friendship might train a person for movements of solidarity, it would be worth pausing over an objection Derrida raises to the conception of friendship that is being presupposed in this discussion. Derrida argues, against Carl Schmitt's insistence on the importance of the political distinction between friend and enemy, that the friend/enemy distinction itself is one that has porous borders, friend becoming enemy and enemy becoming friend, or better friendship becoming enmity and enmity becoming friendship. "The two concepts (friend/enemy) consequently intersect and ceaselessly change places."[23] However, as with all Derridean deconstructions, while the terms pass into each other they are not entirely effaced. If this is true, then the use of friendship to ground the equality of anyone and everyone is a project doomed to failure. There will always be others, even intimate others, who are outside the thematic of friendship we have canvassed here, and thus beyond the capacity to be treated entirely as equals as Rancière would want to have it. Or better, since they would not be entirely beyond that capacity either, we might say more precisely that they would never be entirely on this side of it.

I do not want to claim here that friendship, even friendship strongly characterized by the themes we have described here, is immune to its outside, that is, to some form of enmity. My reasons for reserve, however, are not Derridean but instead have to do with our current context. In a society in which entrepreneurship and consumerism are everywhere pressed upon us, it is unlikely that we can escape their influence, even in our best relationships. My agreement with Derrida on this matter, then (aside from any agreement that would be rooted in the ambivalence of close friendships discussed in the previous chapter) is not on the basis of deconstruction but rather on the basis of our current situation. The question is whether this agreement undercuts the role friendship can play in political solidarity. I believe that it does not. As with my response to the earlier Derridean objection, there is no need to envision a pure friendship in order to envision friendship. Friendship, in its non-economic mode, presses against the figures of neoliberalism, and in doing so presses against neoliberalism itself. It is one thing to admit that this pressing is not pure, that it is surrounded and at times infused by that against which it presses. It is quite another to seek to deconstruct it on that basis. To do the latter is to erase the distinction between the figure of friendship and that of neoliberalism, an erasure that would redound only to the benefit of neoliberalism itself.

Derrida, of course, would not want to accept that neoliberalism would be the beneficiary of a deconstruction of friendship. In his view, the deconstruction leads not to an embrace of neoliberalism but rather to a recognition of democracy as always what he calls a *democracy-to-come*. As he tells us in *Rogues*, "The 'to-come' not only points to the promise but suggests that a democracy will never exist, in the sense of a present existence: not because it will be deferred but because it will always remain aporetic in its structure."[24] What he commends in a deconstruction of the friend-enemy distinction is not an apathy or a yielding to current political relationships, but instead an effacing of the border between friend and enemy that will allow a hospitality to the other to emerge. For Derrida solidarity is created not through the cultivation of friendship but rather through a deconstruction of the borders between the same of friendship and the other of enmity. This would open a space for a recognition of the other that would seem particularly relevant in light of current movements of exclusion of homosexuals, immigrants, etc. Such a space would not be entirely one of differences, nor entirely one of identical equals. It would instead be a space of the economy between the two. As he writes in *Politics of Friendship*, "There is no democracy without respect for irreducible singularity or alterity, but there is no democracy without the 'community of friends' (*koína ta philon*) without the calculation of majorities, without identifiable, stabilizable, representable subjects, all equal. These two laws are irreducible one to the other. Tragically irreconcilable and forever wounding. The wound itself opens with the necessity of having to *count* one's friends, to count the others, in the economy of one's own, there where every other is altogether other."[25]

What we seem to have here, then, is a confrontation of two models of solidarity. One is a broadly Rancièrean model that sees in friendship a model for solidarity, and the other a Derridean model that seeks instead to efface (without, of course, ever entirely erasing) the borders between friendship and enmity. From the perspective of the latter, the former risks excluding others from whatever solidarity is claimed, and thus undercutting the egalitarianism on which it is founded. What is required, from this perspective, is an embrace of a more "messianic" view of democratic solidarity, one that resists bringing to full presence the character, nature, or basis of that solidarity if it wishes to remain democratic. Or, from a different angle, the requirement is to hold together self and other in an unending "tragic" confrontation.

There are, I believe, at least two things that can be said in response to the Derridean perspective, one in defense of Rancière's view and another in criticism of the Derridean alternative. As for the former, the history of nonviolent struggle and teaching suggests that the building of internal solidarity does not require an exclusion of the other. To see the other as an adversary is not to see them as less than equal, or as prohibited in principle from the group to which one belongs. Trouble begins, not when there is resistance but when that resistance hypostasizes the other into an Other, an enemy or a force that must be destroyed or dismantled in order for one to move forward. It is this idea that Martin Luther King captures in a Christain vein when he writes that the doctrine of nonviolent action "was not a doctrine that made their followers yearn for revenge but one that called upon them to champion change. It was not a doctrine that asked an eye for an eye but one that summoned men to seek to open the eyes of blind prejudice. The Negro turned his back on force not only because he knew he could not win his freedom through physical force but also because he believed that through physical force he could lose his soul."[26]

Those who subscribe to Derrida's view might quickly and accurately point out that the adversaries addressed by a Rancièrean view are not the others whom Derrida sees excluded from participation. This is true, and is precisely what leads to the criticism of Derrida's perspective. The deconstructionist view addresses those who are beneficiaries of inequality, those who see themselves as among the *included* rather than the excluded. His discourse seeks to discover (and create) pores in the border the self-perceived included might have erected between themselves and those they exclude. Rancière's view, alternatively, is addressed in the first place to the excluded. It is a framework of solidarity for those who seek to struggle, not for those against whom struggle might be directed.

And, given the dominance of the figures of neoliberalism we have canvassed, the kind of friendship we have outlined here is on the side of the excluded rather than the included. Derrida's deconstruction concerns friendship as a movement of internal cohesion among those who would keep at bay what Rancière calls "the part that has no part."[27] In a neoliberal world, friendship as a movement of internal cohesion can only be one of investment and consumption. At its most cohesive, friendship would be a mutual investment in a collective organization whose goal is to ensure the dominance of those who already have a part. There is no place for friendship as solidarity, because such friendship can only be threatening to the neoliberal order, for reasons we have seen. Thus, the possibilities of friendship that we have outlined here are not properly the subject of a deconstruction but, if anything, part of the other that is to have a space opened for it by a deconstruction. In attempting to deconstruct friendship, then, Derrida is looking through the wrong end of the telescope. In the name of opening a space for the other, he deconstructs one of the social tools by which that space can be opened. The reason he does this is that his discourse, by addressing itself to those who have a part rather than those who lack it, sees friendship only through the eyes of those for whom solidarity is a threat rather than a promise.

So far we have discussed elements in the character of a deep friendship that can provide the basis for, or intersect with, movements of resistance to neolibealism. In addition to providing these thematic elements, close friendships can also provide what might be called training for movements of solidarity. This training is not specific to movements that are opposed specifically to neoliberalism or its effects. It is broader than that; it is training for being in a movement. However, because of the individualizing effects of neoliberalism, friendship provides an important and perhaps even necessary ground for living the kinds of relationships that overcome individual isolation in favor of collective solidarity. In particular, friendship can provide a training in a trust that, as we have seen, is anathema to neoliberal practice.

In a recent article entitled "Fetishizing Process," Mark Lance intervenes in the traditional debate among anarchists regarding whether voting or consensus respects the equality of participants. This debate pits those who think that consensus is more egalitarian because it respects the views of every participant against those who opt for voting because consensus allows any single member to block a group's decision and thereby fail to respect the equality of all participants. Lance argues that this focus on formal group process misses the significance of the training and self-training of the participants themselves. His claim is that we often expect to design processes that will guarantee respect for persons when in fact the processes themselves only work when that respect has been instilled. "An anti-authoritarian democratic organization must not understand itself as defined by a set of formal procedures. Rules can be used, as tools of a virtuous community with a largely functional practice, but they should be no more than tools."[28] What needs to be cultivated instead are the kinds of people that can recognize and respect others, even where they disagree with them, that is, group solidarity.

Friendship provides precisely this training in recognition and respect. It does so through the mechanism of trust. When one trusts another, as we have seen, one makes oneself vulnerable to her. That can only happen if one believes that the other will not abuse one's vulnerability, that the other is both capable and willing not to take advantage of the position one has put oneself in, in short that the other takes responsibility for the trust placed in her. All of this runs counter to the individualism fostered by neoliberalism. More pointedly, however, it allows for the bonds between people necessary to solidarity to develop. I can only be in solidarity with those I trust. Friendship trains me in that trust, and in doing so trains me to interact with others in a common project even where I may disagree with them. This in turn develops the "virtues" Lance notes are necessary for anti-authoritarian democratic organizations, or, for that matter, any democratic organization of solidarity (which, as Rancière would undoubtedly insist, is necessarily anti-authoritarian).

The idea that friendship provides training for solidarity may strike some readers as running counter to the necessarily limited scope of friendship, and especially of deep friendship. Above, in beginning to argue for friendship's relevance to resisting neoliberalism, I conceded that it is not the entirety of friendship that contributes to this resistance, but only certain aspects of it. This is because one cannot be close friends with everyone. If it were required that everyone in a solidarity movement were close friends, there could be no such movements. One might wonder here whether the training I am speaking of here requires everyone in a movement to be close friends. After all, if the recognition and respect in which people are trained is rooted in trust, and if deep trust can only happen among deep friends, could it be that the training for solidarity can only happen among those who are willing to be deep friends with one another?

This discomfort rests on the assumption that in training to place trust in others, one must trust them to the extent one trusts a close or deep friend. If that were the case, solidarity would indeed be difficult, if not impossible. However, that level of trust is not required. In having a close friendship, I learn to trust another human being, to place myself in her hands in important ways. This teaches me that I can approach others as more than centers of competition or objects of personal gain or entertainment. And in working alongside those with whom I have a common interest—which is the case with solidarity movements—I can carry this lesson with me. I can display a readiness to trust others, to respect them, that stems from my experience with my close friends but need not rise to the level of that experience. In learning to trust through my friendships, I need not learn that all trust is of one kind or one level or one intensity. The lesson is more nuanced. I learn how to go about the commitment to trusting others. I learn what it is like, how it works, what I can do to foster it, what some of its limits are, and how to move within a context of trust. All of this I am trained in through the development of close friendships, but none of it is required to reach the level of these friendships in order for me to be in solidarity with others.

In a recent article on gender and friendship, Stephen Marks distinguishes between what he calls "exclusive" and "inclusive" intimacy. His distinction is worth quoting in full:

I suggest that people will be most eager to bridge their separate worlds when their cultural context encourages them to see themselves as unique and private individuals, in possession of important, separate identities. . . In this case, exclusive intimacy will be the preferred pattern, and disclosure work may become quite complex and elaborate, at times including emotional aspects of one's inner experience. However, if people see and experience themselves not as unique individuals but as members of categories or groups (in large part because this is how they are treated by others), then inclusive intimacy will be their preferred pattern. In this latter case, disclosure accounts may be limited to reports of one's "outside" activities and to storytelling about others. Comfort will be drawn more from being surrounded by members of one's group or category than by seeking exclusive ties in which one can fully disclose the finely elaborated inner world of thoughts and feelings.[29]

Inclusive intimacy, which Marks exemplifies through a discussion of a group of female factory workers, is characteristic of solidarity movements. Participants in these movements rarely share intimate details about their lives. They don't generally discuss their hopes, their regrets, or their unfulfilled longings unless a deep friendship develops independent of the movement itself. (Actually, I have been in a number of solidarity movements, and there are some people who do seek to discuss these things in the context of the movement itself. These are people to be avoided.) Nevertheless, there develops a trust among participants that, while it has borders, is solidly constructed within those borders.

One might wonder, looking at the passage from Marks, whether inclusive intimacy is more like Little's social friendship, while exclusive intimacy is more akin to communicating friendship. This surface impression would be misleading on both ends of the analogy. Communicating friendship does not require the level of exclusivity Marks indicates is characteristic of exclusive intimacy. As he notes, exclusivity is fostered by certain cultural contexts rather than by the nature of the friendship itself. More relevant for our purposes, however, is that inclusive intimacy cannot be assimilated to social friendship. Social friendship hews to current interpersonal norms. It does not question or challenge the social arrangements in the way communicating friendship might. The women Marks studied, factory workers who were not unionized nor politically informed, were themselves able to play at the borders of accepted gender roles in their relationships with one another. "Those who remained single needed only to expand their boundaries to include their married friends' husbands and children. . . Through real or fictive kinship, single women became 'aunts' and had children to fuss over. Through domestic partnerships, two sisters got included as a couple in ritual gatherings and festive celebrations among married women. . . And, through working together, all the women elaborated a common work culture."[30]

What Marks describes is neither social nor communicating friendships, but instead a group culture that borrows elements from each. It has the conversational superficiality of social friendships but with a deeper level of trust, a level that approaches—without ever entirely reaching—that of communicating or deep friendship. This group culture is characteristic of many groups in conflict with the larger social order, with what Rancière calls the police order. One can find companionship in these groups that offers an affirmation often denied by the world outside of them. And this would be true also of solidarity movements, since, after all, they are struggling against something that is already in place, something that is either supported or at least taken for granted by a large segment of society. In all of this, we can see the development of interpersonal trust. And this trust, in turn, can be more easily developed when one has experience with it, an experience one finds in the cultivation of close friendships.

The argument I am offering here does not deny two claims held by those who are skeptical of the relevance of friendship for politics. First, it recognizes that deep friendships can be self-enclosed in a way that would be inimical to political solidarity. This self-enclosure does not seem to me, however, to be necessary. There are themes in close friendships, especially their presupposition of equality but also their greater willingness to challenge social norms, that open out onto a flourishing participation in political movements. This is crucial in the neoliberal period, where equality and social solidarity are discouraged in favor of individualism. Second, the argument recognizes that in such movements one cannot be friends with everyone. On the other hand, I have insisted that the training involved in a deep friendship, and in particular the training in trust, is relevant for learning how to assimilate oneself into a solidarity movement. Those who have learned to cultivate close friendships are more, rather than less, likely to be able to immerse themselves in movements that require a solid, if not intimate, bond among participants.

If deep friendships provide both themes and training for movements of political resistance to neoliberalism, they provide a third element as well: motivation. The motivation to resist neoliberalism can come from a variety of sources: its economic effects, its concentration of power into fewer hands, its denial of efficacy to representative political institutions. All of these are reasonable motivations to challenge the hegemony of neoliberal thought and practice. However, there is another motivation for challenging neoliberalism, one that lies closer to its effects on this book's theme: close friendship. In the previous chapter, we saw the kinds of friendships neoliberalism fosters and encourages. These are friendships of pleasure and friendships of profit. We don't want to claim that the existence of such friendships *in themselves* is deleterious for the development of deep friendships. On the contrary, in order for societies to function there have to be ways for people to cooperate in a friendly manner without having to become close friends. Whether we call certain relationships friendships of pleasure or social friendships, and others friendships of usefulness or familiar friendships (recalling that these analogies do not map exactly onto each other), we can readily concede the important roles they have to play in maintaining social cooperation and even promoting individual development.

The difficulty comes in what we discussed above in this chapter. The context constructed by neoliberalism does not simply promote friendships like these *alongside* close friendships; it promotes them *instead of* such friendships. This is because neoliberalism seeks to construct an environment defined by individualism and a lack of trust. Such an environment is not only different from that in which deep friendships can flourish; it actively discourages their development.

It is important to be clear about the dynamic of neoliberalism in this regard. It is not, as we saw, because neoliberalism consciously intends to interfere with close friendships that it constructs an environment that is anathema to their development. Neoliberalism is the dominance of certain practices and their corresponding ways of thinking. There is nothing, strictly speaking, that neoliberalism can intend, since there is nobody named Neoliberalism to intend it. Nor is it that those who direct or benefit from the dominant practices of neoliberalism intend to discourage the emergence of deep friendships. In all likelihood, many if not most of those people have deep friendships of their own. Rather, the problem is that the practices and institutions of neoliberalism are accompanied by ways of thinking about ourselves and our relationships that run counter to those ways of thinking that allow us to open ourselves to such friendships. Inasmuch as we think of ourselves as consumers and entrepreneurs, and act in accordance with these self-conceptions, we are unlikely to open ourselves to close friendships. They will not appear to us as possibilities on our interpersonal horizon.

And this gives us a motivation to resist the infiltration of neoliberalism into our lives. If we are to be able to maintain a set of relationships that lend our lives the meaning they do, and if we are to enable those who follow us to do so, we must—and more to the point we will want to—challenge neoliberalism at the level of its effects on our relationships. We will want to protect both the relationships and the atmosphere that allows them to arise from the encroachment of the figures of neoliberalism. We will want to ensure that those we care about, and that we ourselves, do not become subject to neoliberal self-conceptions.

One might argue at this point that, to the extent to which neoliberalism already dominates us, it is too late to introduce this motivation. If we already think of ourselves in the terms neoliberalism sets out for us, if we already are figures of neoliberalism, from where would the motivation come to think of ourselves differently? To the extent to which we have been formed by neoliberalism, such a motivation would already be sapped, or perhaps channeled into the development of relationships that are more in accordance with the figures of neoliberalism. Resistance needs a source. What would be the source of motivation to resist what we already are? Since we are already that thing, would we not accept, would we not lack the very terms to reject it?

To this argument, we must have a twofold response. First, we are not already that thing. As we have seen, although neoliberalism pervades our culture, it has not overtaken us. Many, if not most, of us have deep friendships. We also likely to have other aspects of our lives that are not in thrall to the figures of the consumer and the entrepreneur. If neoliberalism is the one of the dominant elements in which our lives are immersed, it is not the only element. We might think of it this way. While there are no aspects of our lives that are entirely immune to the influence of neoliberal thought and practice, there are many aspects of our lives that are not entirely pervaded by it either.

We might capture this idea by contrasting two images. It is not that there are compartments of our lives untouched by neoliberal thought and practice. If the ideas of the first chapter are even nearly right, neoliberalism has had an influence on how we think of ourselves and others. That influence has likely reached into many corners of our lives. Rather than thinking of compartments, we can think in terms of fluids. Neoliberalism has seeped into many aspects of our lives, but its concentration is much lesser in some aspects than in others. For those of us with deep and long-standing friendships, for instance, the influence of neoliberalism is likely to be much less pervasive than it would be in other, more superficial relationships. The issue then is not one of possessing aspects of our lives that are entirely cordoned off from neoliberal influence, but rather of having aspects where its influence is either weak or irrelevant.

This idea allows us to recognize that it would be false, too simplistic, to say that we are already that thing. That thing is with us. It suffuses our lives. But we are—at least most of us are—not exhausted by that thing's influence.

The second part of the response strikes a note of caution. If we are not entirely creatures of neoliberalism, and if our lives are not compartmentalized so that there are aspects of them that it cannot reach, then we must be vigilant. We must ensure that we do not become so pervaded by neoliberal influence that we become that thing, that we become so much the consumer and/or the entrepreneur that these figures define us to our very roots. As we saw in the first chapter, people are always in part, always more or less, creatures of their time. If the effects of neoliberalism are as I have suggested, then the less we are creatures of our particular time, the better. But we cannot simply assume that, in an atmosphere so pervaded by consumerism and entrepreneurship, resistance to these effects will come naturally. This book is, at least in part, an effort to counsel vigilance, and to display an important place in our lives where we might exercise it. But wherever and however we look, look we must. Neoliberalism is not the entirety of who we are. But neither is it entirely outside of us. To recognize the forms it takes, particularly with regard to our lives, and to resist those forms is a task we must consciously take up if we are to ensure that we do not become, to any greater extent than we have to, what it seeks to make of us. Since almost all of us already have aspects of who we are and how we are with others that we value and that run counter to neoliberal themes, we have motivation to engage in that resistance. The trick is to recognize that motivation and to keep it by us.

NOTES

1. Foucault, Michel, "Friendship as a Way of Life," *Foucault Live*, tr. John Johnston, ed. Sylvére Lotinger, (New York: Semiotext(e), 1989), p. 205.

2. Aristotle, *Nichomachean Ethics*, p. 232 (1060a28–30)

3. MacIntyre, Alasdair, *After Virtue: A Study in Moral Theory*, third edition. (Notre Dame: Notre Dame Press, 2007 [1981]), p. 156.

4. Arendt, Hannah, "Socrates," in *The Promise of Politics*, (New York: Schocken Books, 2005 [1990]), pp. 17–18.

5. Allen, Danielle, *Talking to Strangers: Anxieties of Citizenship since* Brown v. Board of Education, (Chicago: University of Chicago Press, 2004), p. 136.

6. Aristotle, *Nichomachean Ethics*, p. 269 (1171a18–20)

7. Derrida, *Politics of Friendship*, tr. George Collins (London: Verso, 1997), p. 21.

8. cf. Lane, *The Loss of Happiness in Market Democracies*, pp. 253–60.

9. Nehamas, "The Good of Friendship," p. 291.

10. "Lecture on Friendship," in Pakaluk, *Other Selves*, pp. 213–14.

11. *Inequality Reexamined* (Cambridge: Harvard University Press, 1992), p. ix.

12. Cf. *The Political Thought of Jacques Rancière: Creating Equalty* and *Contemporary Movements and the Thought of Jacques Rancière: Equality in Action*, both from Edinburgh University Press, 2008 and 2010 respectively.

13. *Disagreement*, p. 28.

14. *Disagreement*, pp. 29–30.

15. Rancière, Jacques, *Disagreement*, tr. Julie Rose (Minneapolis: University of Minnesota Press, 1999), p. 30.

16. Rancière, Jacques, *On the Shores of Politics*, tr. Liz Heron (London: Verso, 1995), p. 61.

17. Rancière, Jacques, *On the Shores of Politics*, tr. Liz Heron. London: Verso, 1995 [1992], pp. 32–33.

18. In fact, that's exactly what I argue in *The Political Thought of Jacques Rancière*.

19. Friedman, Marilyn, "Feminism and Modern Friendship," in Badhwar, Neera Kapur. *Friendship: A Philosophical Reader* (Ithaca: Cornell University Press, 1993), p. 298.

20. See Bhagwati, *In Defense of Globalization*, chapter 7.

21. For an account of export processing zones and women's place in them, see Naomi Klein's *No Logo: Taking Aim at the Brand Bullies* (New York: Picador, 1999), chapter 9.

22. Harvey, p. 170.

23. Derrida, *Politics of Friendship*, p. 72.

24. Derrida, Jaques. *Rogues: Two Essays on Reason*, tr.Brault, Pascale-Anne, and Nass, Michael (Palo Alto: Stanford University Press, 2005), p. 86.

25. Derrida, *Politics of Friendship*, p. 22. We should note here that in this passage Derrida seems to reduce equality to sameness. There is no reason that equality should be thought of in terms of sameness. Although this point would take us too far afield, I address it in the context of Rancière's thought in *The Political Thought of Jacques Rancière: Creating Equality* (Edinburgh and University Park, Edinburgh University Press and Penn State University Press, 2008), pp. 56–64.

26. King, Martin Luther, "The Sword that Heals," in *Why We Can't Wait* (New York: New American Library, 1964), p. 35.

27. Cf. Rancière, *Disagreement*, esp. pp. 8–9.

28. Lance Mark, "Fetishizing Process," Institute for Anarchist Studies, http://zinelibrary.info/files/Fetishizing%20Process.pdf

29. Marks, Stephen R. "The gendered contexts of inclusive intimacy: The Hawthorne women at work and home," in Adams and Allen, *Placing Friendship in Context*, p. 45.

30. Marks, "The gendered contexts of inclusive intimacy," p. 65.

EIGHT

Conclusion

Close friendship provides an alternative to neoliberal influence and can offer several tools that might be utilized in resisting it: the theme of equality (and to a lesser extent the willingness to challenge social norms), the training in trust, and the motivation to preserve meaningful aspects of our lives. All of this makes friendship a fruitful area for reflection in considering how to conduct our lives in the social, political, and economic context in which we find ourselves.

Regarding resistance, it is easy to misunderstand what I have claimed on its behalf. I have not claimed that deep friendships lead naturally to forms of political resistance. As we saw at the outset of this section, friendship can be an exclusive relationship, and in any case it is impossible to be close friends with everyone in a movement of solidarity. It is entirely possible, although not at all necessary, that the cultivation of deep friendships would turn one away from the involvement in more public concerns.

I have not claimed that having close friendships makes us better people. I suspect that the ability to have a close friendship has elements that might lend themselves to this, but I have not argued this. And to argue it would require separating out those elements from other ones, since it is clear to me, as I have argued, that close friendships can occur among deeply flawed or wounded individuals.

Finally, I have not claimed that friendship is the only route to resistance to the influence of neoliberalism. It is simply one route, a route that is often ignored as well as one whose themes can be implicit in other routes. One can imagine a solidarity movement of people who either have no close friends or, more likely, whose close friendships do not inform or train them in their participation. I think this is improbable, since I don't believe we easily cordon off important aspects of our lives from others. But it seems at least possible.

In short, the relation of friendship to political resistance in general and resistance to neoliberalism in particular is doubly contingent. Friendship is not necessary for resistance, and it does not necessarily lead there.

Why bring the two together then?

There are two reasons for this. First, although there are difficulties and tensions between friendship and solidarity, although it is not a clean or seamless relationship, nevertheless friendship can offer themes, training, and motivation for solidarity in general and resistance to neoliberalism in particular. In an age where it is often difficult for people to see their way to solidarity, even when—as many do—they agree that there is much to be resisted in our world, finding sources of solidarity is an important task. Moreover, although the relationship between friendship and solidarity is not straightforward, deep friendship does constitute a straightforward *alternative* to neoliberal relationships. In reflecting on our friendships, then, we might be motivated to resistance by that aspect of friendship alone. This is especially true if we feel the atmosphere in which we can cultivate those friendships to be threatened.

Second, friendship is not far to seek. Almost all of us have deep friendships of one kind or another. Inasmuch as these deep friendships provide a source for solidarity, we do not have to look far in our world to discover a site from which we can draw nourishment. As I mentioned a couple of times in this book, I have many students who recognize that there is something profoundly awry in the way the world is currently arranged, but who feel helpless to do something about it. They have a sense neither of hope nor of vision. Deep friendships can assist in providing both. They provide vision because they encompass elements of the kinds of relationships one would like to see in a world more just. They provide hope in the fact that neoliberalism has not overtaken all that is worthy in human relationships. When I discuss friendship in the context of resistance with my students, they recognize it as a source at least for reflection on conceptions of a better world.

All of this is more difficult, however, if we fail to recognize the role deep friendship plays in our lives and the possibilities it offers to resist what is inimical to our flourishing together. What I have sought to accomplish here is to place that role and those possibilities in front of us. We cannot aspire to, much less intend, a better world when we cannot see beyond the throes of this one. Friendship, we can come to realize, is a wellspring for that aspiration. Not the only one, to be sure, but one that is rooted in what is among the most meaningful aspects of our lives.

Appendix: Virtual Friendships

In the December 11, 2009, issue of *The Chronicle Review*, the writer William Deresiewicz published an article entitled "Faux Friendship," which decried the effect of social networking sites, especially Facebook, on friendship. "Friendship is devolving, in other words, from a relationship to a feeling—from something people share to something each of us hugs privately to ourselves in the loneliness of our electronic caves, rearranging the tokens of connection like a lonely child playing with dolls."[1] He traces a history of friendship that recounts the heroic friendships of the pre-modern period to the democratic friendships and then group friendships of the modern period to the virtual friendships of the past several years. The advent of MySpace in 2003 and Facebook in 2004 seems to betray the character of friendship. It substitutes a personal sharing of information for interpersonal connection. The shared time and conversation necessary for friendship has been replaced by the posting of quirks about oneself and the commenting on one another's walls. "We have given our hearts to machines," he concludes, "and now we are turning into machines."[2]

Nicholas Christakis and James Fowler, in their book *Connected*, offer a very different perspective. They see the technology of communication as bringing people closer together. Taking a historical perspective, they argue that the same worries that are currently being expressed about virtual connections were once expressed about the telephone. "Many worried that domestic life would be constantly interrupted. . . . There were also concerns about loss of privacy. . . . Others thought that rushed telephone conversations would be socially dangerous, as 'speakers cannot prepare for or reflect upon the discussion as they can in letters'. . . and observers worried about the ways in which the telephone would change courtship rituals, leading to inappropriate sexual contact."[3] These worries seem anachronistic to us now, as the authors feel the worries about the Internet will seem in the future.

In support of their view, they cite a study in the late 1990s of a suburb of Toronto where free broadband technology was offered to all residents, and where 60 percent of the residents chose to utilize it. The study revealed that, "Residents who had access to these services developed deeper and broader connections to other residents, with more neighborhood ties."[4] Not only were there more connections among the residents who used the technology, those residents were also more involved in the civic life of the community than those who forsook the technology. There are, of course, other explanations for these results than the technology. Perhaps, for instance, many of those who declined the services were people who did not want as much connection with others as those who accepted it. However, it seems at least that the virtual connections among the residents did not result in a decline of interpersonal interaction.

This study was conducted before the rise of MySpace and Facebook, and one might wonder what effects, if any, their existence would have had. However, the debate between Deresiewicz and Christakis and Fowler as to the effects of virtual communication media on friendships reflects a larger divide between those who think that virtual communication is deleterious for friendship and healthy social interaction generally and those who think it fosters and enhances them.

The rise of Facebook and other virtual social media is likely to have significant effects on friendship. I don't think we know what those effects are yet, though. As I write this, Facebook is only seven years old. I suspect as well that part of the explanation for the strong reactions pro and contra virtual connections lies precisely in the fact that we don't know their effects. There is a sense that these media will have a significant impact on our cultural and interpersonal lives, but we do not yet understand what those effects are or will be. As a result, many people either rush to embrace or to reject these media.

At this point, I do not feel prepared to add very much to this discussion. It seems to me premature to pronounce on phenomena like Facebook, or upon the general consequences of virtual social media on friendships. This is why I have left this theme to this short appendix. Given our discussion of friendship, there are perhaps a few things we can say to frame thought about virtual social media. But an understanding of what happens in the frame will have to await another book and probably another author.

Deep friendships are rooted in shared activities and conversation. As we have seen, close friends accrete time together in which they develop (or emerge from) common interests, and in which they deepen their relationship through interpersonal discussion and mutual growth. This does not seem to preclude virtual interaction, but does raise questions about interaction that is *solely* virtual. For an example of the former, we can take email. Deresiewicz is leery of email interaction. "E-mail," he writes, "with its rapid-fire etiquette and scrolling format, already trimmed a letter down to a certain acceptable maximum, perhaps a thousand words."[5] The comparison of email to letters, however, may be misleading.

It is certainly true that letters are more reflective, usually considered and written at a leisurely pace and often longer than email. However, it may be that the role of email in a friendship is different from that of letters. Rather than being central to the development of a friendship, email can serve to sustain it during periods of geographic distance. It can be more like a series of quick phone conversations, where people keep up with what one another is doing rather than communicating in Little's sense or developing evaluative outlooks. (Of course, email serves a number of purposes, many of them professional. Those are not our concern here.) In this way, email is less an impoverished form of a letter and more like a postcard. And it has several advantages over postcards: it doesn't take very long to get to its recipient, it is easy to send more of them than of postcards, and it's cheaper. In a world in which friends are often living in different cities, email offers a sense of regular connection that can help nourish a friendship during those periods (often long ones) of forced physical separation.

Seen this way, email is a supplement to the central elements of a deep friendship. It rarely plays the role of developing the themes of such friendships discussed above. This leaves open the question of whether virtual communication can indeed serve as a medium through which close friendships can develop. Can email or social media websites do more than subsidize or fortify an already existing friendship? Can the virtual world provide something that can substitute for the shared actual time that friends spend together?

Again, it is too early to know. If the approach offered to deep friendship here is right, however, there are at least two hurdles that need to be cleared in order for virtual friendships to be able to substitute for offline friendships. The first is shared activity. Dereisiewicz complains that, with Facebook, "information replaces experience, as it has throughout our culture."[6] Rather than undergo experiences with friends, Facebook, in his view, is nothing more than posting information about oneself. If this is true, it would reflect the individualism characteristic of the two figures of neoliberalism. It would likely tilt the relationships formed on social networking sites either to the consumerist as a form of entertainment or the entrepreneurial as people sought out others as a means of forming useful connections. Is this true, however? Are social networking sites devoid of shared experience?

There are legitimate worries here. In shared face-to-face experience, people do something together. They engage in a common activity, whether it be athletic, conversational, political, or otherwise. They build a shared life. Moreover, by building that shared life in each other's or one another's presence they engage in what might be called the eroticism of their bodies. By this I don't mean anything particularly sexual. The eroticism of friends' bodies is the enjoyment of being around friends, seeing their facial expressions, hearing their voices, perhaps occasionally hugging them or touching their arm. One enjoys the corporeal presence of friends. The question that arises for friendships that are exclusively virtual is whether the kinds of activities that occur online are robust enough for sustaining a deep friendship, and whether the lack of physical presence constitutes a bar to forming a bond of the type that distinguishes those kinds of friendships.

Related to this, we have seen that close friendships are rooted in the history of time shared together. It is not merely the present in its occurrence or the future in its prospect that defines such a friendship. The past as it is sedimented in the relationship both orients and gives heft to the relationship among good friends. The question this raises for virtual friendship is whether there is something capable of playing this role in virtual relationships. Deresiewicz writes that, "Facebook holds out a utopian possibility: What once was lost will now be found. But the heaven of the past is a promised land destroyed in the reaching. Facebook, here, becomes the anti-madeleine, an eraser of memory."[7]

Deresiewicz is right to point to the importance of the past in constituting deep friendships. And he is right to insist that the past is not simply a matter of bringing forward images or memories that have no vital connection with the present. But it seems too early to declare virtual social networks as incapable of a more robust integration of past and present. There are difficulties, to be sure, among them the obstacle of shared activities that could constitute a common past. Whether, in the end, these difficulties will be overcome in the evolution of Facebook or other social websites is a matter for the future (and our reflective vigilance) to decide. It is worth recognizing the requirements of a deep friendship, in order that we not sacrifice some of our most meaningful relations on the altar of technology. By the same token, however, it seems premature to pronounce upon technology as incapable of sustaining those relationships. It is probably uncontroversial to say that recent communication technologies can assist in the maintenance of previously existing friendships, especially in a world in which people often find themselves further flung from one another than they would choose to be. Whether and to what degree those same technologies can actually create such friendships is, I believe, a matter about which we do not have the answer. And, lacking the answer, we should be at once open to the possibilities for friendship that they might offer and wary about the dangers they present.

NOTES

1. Deresiewicz, William, "Faux Friendship," *The Chronicle Review*, December 11, 2009, p. B9.
2. Deresiewicz, "Faux Friendship," p. B10.
3. Christakis, Nicholas A. and Fowler, James H., *Connected: The Surprising Power of Our Social Networks and How They Shape Our Lives* (New York: Little, Brown and Co., 2009), p. 267.
4. Christakis and Fowler, *Connected*, p. 269.
5. Deresiewicz, "Faux Friends," p. B10.
6. Deresiewicz, "Faux Friends," p. B10.
7. Deresiewicz, "Faux Friends," p. B10.

Bibliography

Adams, Rebecca G., and Allan, Graham. "Contextualizing Friendship," in Adams, Rebecca G., and Allan, Graham, *Placing Friendship in Context*. Cambridge: Cambridge University Press, 1998.

Allen, Danielle. *Talking to Strangers: Anxieties of Citizenship since* Brown v. Board of Education. Chicago: University of Chicago Press, 2004.

Arendt, Hannah. "Socrates," in *The Promise of Politics*. New York: Schocken Books, 2005 [1990].

Aristotle. *Nicomachean Ethics*, tr. Martin Oswald. Indianapolis: Bobbs-Merrill, 1962.

Barber, Benjamin. *Con$umed: How Markets Corrupt Children, Infantilize Adults, and Swallow Citizens Whole*. New York: W.W. Norton, 2007.

Bauman, Zygmunt. *Consuming Life*. Cambridge: Polity Press, 2007.

———. *Liquid Love: On the Frailty of Human Bonds*. Cambridge: Polity Press, 2003.

———. *Liquid Modernity*. Cambridge: Polity Press, 2000.

Becker, Gary. "An Economic Analysis of Fertility," in *The Economic Approach to Human Behavior* Chicago: University of Chicago Press, 1976.

———. "The Economic Way of Looking at Life," http://home.uchicago.edu/gbecker/Nobel/nobellecture.pdf , 1992.

———. *Human Capital*, Third edition. Chicago: University of Chicago Press, 1993.

———. "A Theory of the Allocation of Time," *The Economic Journal*, Vol. 75, No. 299, September 1965.

Becker, Gary. *A Treatise on the Family*. Cambridge: Harvard University Press, 1981

Bhagwati, Jagdish. *In Defense of Globalization*. Oxford: Oxford University Press, 2004

Brewer, Talbot. *The Retrieval of Ethics*. Oxford: Oxford University Press, 2009

Bronner, Ethan. "College Students Aiming for High Marks in Income," *New York Times*, January 12, 1998, http://query.nytimes.com/gst/fullpage.html?res=9901E3DE1539F931A25752C0A96E958260&scp=2&sq=college%20students%20%22meaningful%20philosophy%20of%20life%22&st=cse (accessed December 6, 2010)

Brown, Wendy "Neoliberalism and the End of Liberal Democracy," in *Edgework: Critical Essays on Knowledge and Politics* Princeton: Princeton University Press, 2005.

Burge, Tyler. "Individualism and the Mental," *Midwest Studies in Philosophy*, Vol. 4, No. 1, 1979.

Cassidy, John. "What Good is Wall Street?" *The New Yorker*, November 29, 2010.

Chang, Ha-Joon. *Bad Samaritans: The Myth of Free Trade and the Secret History of Capitalism*. London: Bloomsbury Press, 2008.

Christakis, Nicholas A. and Fowler, James H. *Connected: The Surprising Power of Our Social Networks and How They Shape Our Lives* (New York: Little, Brown and Co., 2009).

Cicero. "On Friendship," in Pakaluk, Michael (ed.), *Other Selves: Philosophers on Friendship* Indianapolis: Hackett, 1991.

Davis, Mike. *Planet of Slums*. London: Verso Press, 2006.

Deresiewicz, William. "Faux Friendship," *The Chronicle Review*, December 11, 2009.

Derrida, Jacques. *Given Time: 1. Counterfeit Money*, tr. Peggy Kamuf. Chicago: University of Chicago Press, 1992 [1991].

———. *Politics of Friendship*, tr. George Collins. London: Verso, 1997 [1994].

———. *Rogues: Two Essays on Reason*, tr. Brault, Pascale-Anne, and Nass, Michael. Palo Alto: Stanford University Press, 2005 [2003].

Descartes, René, *Philosophical Essays and Correspondence.* ed. Roger Ariew. Indianapolis: Hackett, 2000.

Dickens, Charles, *Great Expectations.* New York: New American Library, 1963 [1867].

Ewald, François. *L'Etat Providence.* Paris: Bernard Grasset, 1986

Feld, Scott, and Carter, William C. "Foci of activity as changing contexts for friendship," in Adams, Rebecca G., and Allan, Graham, *Placing Friendship in Context.* Cambridge: Cambridge University Press, 1998.

Foucault, Michel. *Abnormal: Lectures at the Collège de France 1974-1975.* Tr. Graham Burchell. New York: Picador, 2003 [1999].

———. *The Birth of Biopolitics: Lectures at the Collège de France, 1978–1979.* Tr. Graham Burchell. New York: Palgrave Macmillan, 2008 [2004].

———. *Discipline and Punish: The Birth of the Prison.* Tr. Alan Sheridan. New York: Random House, 1977 [1975].

———. "Friendship as a Way of Life," *Foucault Live,* tr. John Johnston, ed. Sylvére Lotinger. New York: Semiotext(e), 1989.

———. *The History of Sexuality, Vol. 1: An Introduction.* Tr. Robert Hurley. New York: Random House, 1980 [1978].

———. "So is it important to think?" In J. Faubion (ed.). Tr. Robert Hurley and others. *Power The Essential Works of Michel Foucault 1954-1984. Volume Three.* New York: New Press, 2000.

Freeman, Alan. "Globalisation: Economic stagnation and divergence," in Pettifor, *A Real World Economic Outlook,* Basingstoke: Palgrave MacMillan, 2003, pp. 152–59.

Friedman, Marilyn. "Feminism and Modern Friendship," in Badhwar, Neera Kapur. *Friendship: A Philosophical Reader.* Ithaca: Cornell University Press, 1993.

Friedman, Milton. *Capitalism and Freedom.* Chicago: University of Chicago Press, 1962.

———. "The Social Responsibility of Business is to Increase its Profits." *New York Times Magazine,* September 13, 1970.

Grau, Christopher, "Irreplaceability and Unique Value," *Philosophical Topics,* Vols. 1 and 2, 2004.

———. "Love and History," *The Southern Journal of Philosophy,* Vol. 48 No. 3.

Harvey, David. *A Brief History of Neoliberalism,* Oxford: Oxford University Press, 2005.

Hinchman, Edward. "Telling as Inviting to Trust," *Philosophy and Phenomenological Research,* Vol. 70, No. 3, May 2005.

Johansen, Robert. *The National Interest and the Human Interest: An Analysis of U.S. Foreign Policy.* Princeton: Princeton University Press, 1980.

Johnston, David Cay. "'04 Income in U.S. Was Below 2000 Level," *New York Times,* November 28, 2006, http://www.nytimes.com/2006/11/28/business/28tax.html?_r=1 (accessed December 14, 2010).

Kant, Immanuel. "Lecture on Friendship," in Pakaluk, Michael (ed.), *Other Selves: Philosophers on Friendship.* Indianapolis: Hackett, 1991.

Kauppinen, Antti. "Meaningfulness and Time," *Philosophy and Phenomenological Research,* Early View, http://onlinelibrary.wiley.com.proxy.lib.clemson.edu/doi/10.1111/j.1933-1592.2010.00490.x/full (accessed July 27, 2011).

Keating, M. F. "Globalisation and the Dynamics of Impoverishment," http://www.richmond.ac.uk/cms/pdfs/Keating%202001%20DSA%20Paper%20PDF.pdf (accessed October 12, 2010).

Keynes, John Maynard. *The General Theory of Employment, Money, and Interest.* London: Macmillan, 2007 [1936].

King, Martin Luther. "The Sword that Heals," in *Why We Can't Wait.* New York: New American Library, 1964.

Klein, Naomi. *No Logo: Taking Aim at the Brand Bullies.* New York: Picador, 1999.

———. *The Shock Doctrine: The Rise of Disaster Capitalism.* New York: Metropolitan Books, 2007.

Lance Mark. "Fetishizing Process," Institute for Anarchist Studies, http://zinelibrary.info/files/Fetishizing%20Process.pdf

Lane, Robert E. *The Loss of Happiness in Market Democracies*. New Haven: Yale University Press, 2000.

———. *The Market Experience*. Cambridge: Cambridge University Press, 1991.

Layard, Richard. *Happiness: Lessons from a New Science*. New York: Penguin Press, 2005.

Little, Graham. *Friendship: Being Ourselves with Others*, Melbourne: Scribe Publications: 2000.

MacIntyre, Alasdair. *After Virtue: A Study in Moral Theory*, Third Edition. Notre Dame: Notre Dame Press, 2007 [1981].

Marfleet, Phil. "Globalisation and the Third World," http://pubs.socialistreviewindex.org.uk/isj81/marfleet.htm (accessed October 12, 2010).

Marks, Stephen R. "The gendered contexts of inclusive intimacy: the Hawthorne women at work and home," in Adams, Rebecca G., and Allan, Graham, *Placing Friendship in Context*. Cambridge: Cambridge University Press, 1998.

Mauss, Marcel. *The Gift: The form and reason for exchange in archaic societies*. Tr. W. D. Halls. New York: W.W. Norton, 1990 [1950].

May, Todd. *Contemporary Movements and the Thought of Jacques Rancière: Equality in Action*. Edinburgh: Edinburgh University Press, 2010.

———. *The Political Thought of Jacques Rancière: Creating Equality*. Edinburgh: Edinburgh University Press, 2008.

Miyoshi, Masao. "A Borderless World? From Colonialism to Transnationalism and the Decline of the Nation-State," *Critical Inquiry*, Vol. 19, Summer 1993.

Montopoli, Brian, "Tea Party Supporters: Who They Are and What They Believe," *CBS News*, http://www.cbsnews.com/8301-503544_162-20002529-503544.html (accessed December 14, 2010).

Moran, Richard. "Getting Told and Being Believed," *Philosopher's Imprint*, Vol. 5, No. 5, August 2005.

Nehamas, Alexander. "The Good of Friendship," *Proceedings of the Aristotelian Society*, Vol. 90, Part 3, October 2010.

Pahl, Ray. *On Friendship*. London: Polity Press, 2000.

Posner, Richard. *Sex and Reason*. Cambridge: Harvard University Press, 1992.

Prasad, Eswar, Rogoff, Kenneth, Wei, Shang-Jin, and Kose, M. Ayan. "Effects of Financial Globalization on Developing Countries: Some Empirical Evidence," www.imf.org/external/np/res/docs/2003/031703.pdf, (accessed October 12, 2010).

Rancière, Jacques. *Disagreement*, tr. Julie Rose, Minneapolis: University of Minnesota Press, 1999 [1995].

———. *On the Shores of Politics*. tr. Liz Heron. London: Verso, 1995 [1992].

Rokeach, Milton. "Change and Stability in American Value Systems: 1968–1971," *Public Opinion Quarterly*, Vol. 38, 1978.

Rokeach, Milton. and Ball-Rokeach, Sandra J. "Stability and Change in American Value Priorities, 1968–1981," *American Psychologist*, Vol. 44, 1989.

Schor, Juliet B. *Born to Buy: The Commercialized Child and the New Consumer Culture*. New York: Scribner, 2004.

Schultz, Theodore. *Human Resources*. New York: National Bureau of Economic Research, 1972.

———. "Investment in Man: An Economic View," *The Social Service Review*, Vol. 33, No. 2, June 1959.

Sen, Amartya. *Inequality Reexamined*. Cambridge: Harvard University Press, 1992.

Simons, Henry. "A Positive Program for Lassez Faire: Some Proposals for a Liberal Economic Policy," in Simons, Henry, *Economic Policy for a Free Society*. Chicago: University of Chicago Press, 1948.

Spencer, Liz, and Pahl, Ray. *Rethinking Friendship: Hidden Solidarities Revealed*. Princeton: Princeton University Press, 2006.

Stiglitz, Joseph. *Globalization and its Discontents*. New York: W.W. Norton, 2002.

Telfer, Elizabeth, "Friendship," in Pakaluk, Michael (ed.), *Other Selves: Philosophers on Friendship*, Indianapolis: Hackett, 1991 [1971].

Veroff, Joseph, Douvan, Elizabeth and Kalka, Richard A. *The Inner Americans: A Self-Portrait from 1957 to 1976*, New York: Basic Books, 1981.

Weber, Max. "'Objectivity' in Social Science and Social Policy," in Weber, Max, *The Methodology of the Social Sciences*. Ed. Edward A. Shils and Henry A. Finch. New York: Free Press, 1949.

Wolf, Susan. *Meaning in Life and Why it Matters*. Princeton: Princeton University Press, 2010.

Index

Made in the USA
Las Vegas, NV
13 April 2021